TRAVEL GUIDE

Guaranteed good times in thirty great Montana towns

By Kent Harris

GOOD TIMES PUBLISHING

Goodtimes Publications
P.O. Box 10
Absarokee, Montana 59001

Additional books may be ordered at the above address for a cost of $9.95 each. Please include a personal check with order.

Dedication

To the thirty pioneers
who contributed to this first edition
of Delightful Detours

Table of Contents

Forward

Delightful Detours was written for travelers who are ready for something more than Disneyland, Las Vegas or the Edmonton Mall. People everywhere are discovering that small towns offer a uniquely satisfying way to get away from it all. Somehow trying to find a really enjoyable destination for anything from a weekend jaunt to a three week vacation becomes more difficult all the time. Much of traveling has become a matter of trying to avoid bad experiences that seem inevitable these days. Delightful Detours tries to help by giving you specific advice on where to go to find a great meal, a clean motel or some interesting shopping in thirty great Montana communities. We want to take the risk out of getting off the Interstate and offer you a chance to savor a wonderfully relaxing and rewarding way to travel. If you are tired of high prices, hassles and unfriendliness so common with traditional get-a-ways, I think you'll enjoy what we have to offer.

Much of what's best about America is still alive and well in our small towns. Those of us who live in rural communities enjoy a quality of life many feel is second to none. Travelers quickly sense what it's all about when they pull into a parking spot right in front of their destination....walk away from their unlocked car for a leisurely stroll down an uncongested sidewalk....enjoy great personal service from a clerk or waitress who takes the time to smile, offers some friendly conversation and even advice on where to find the local attractions....sit down for a first class meal for well under $10....check into a clean, quiet motel for $40.....even get the phone number of a local resident who is ready, willing and able to help you find what you're looking for. This is what you'll experience in Montana's small towns. This is what the guaranteed goodtimes guide is designed to help you find.

I tried hard to avoid lists and statistics. I want readers to sense what Montana has to offer in a guide filled with personal recommendations and anecdotes, not a directory of all the places to get pizza in Plentywood. A few brave souls in thirty communities contributed by sharing their insights into a few of the people, places and events that make them special. Because "Delightful Detours" was a new and untested publication, many towns we contacted chose not to participate. That's why you may not see the community you are looking for. This turned out to be a blessing for me as publishing a 140 page guide covering thirty communities was plenty for the first effort. Likewise, because I felt a strong desire to avoid lists and I wanted local contributors to offer recommendations they would make to a visiting friend, many great places and events were left out. I wanted the guide to be a sampling of places and events of possible interest in each community, not a comprehensive list. For those who do offer a guaranteed goodtime and weren't included, I offer my apologies. I would like to tell our readers about you in our next issue. For readers who had a good experience at a place that wasn't included, please drop me a note telling me about it. I will be updating the guide for future editions and would appreciate your input. Lastly I want to apologize to any students of the English language who might pick up the guide. I tried to use a style that would allow a lot of information to be conveyed in a conversational manner with the least amount of punctuation. I do carry the use of run on sentences and misplaced modifiers to new heights.

Additional books can be ordered at $9.95 each by writing me at Box 10, Absarokee, Mt 59001. I hope you enjoy life a little more because of the guide and I wish you peace.

Kent Harris

BIGFORK

An interesting stop in western Montana, Bigfork has been seen through many eyes—Indians, trappers, loggers, farmers, tourists—even labeled one of the 50 great towns in the West by author David Vokac. Straddling the Swan River where it flows into the sparkling blue Flathead Lake, Bigfork offers an easygoing village lifestyle complimented by lots of urban amenities: Broadway musicals (performed by one of the Northwest's finest repertory theaters), Sunday concerts in the park, fine art galleries and gourmet dining. All this along with an extraordinary diversity of recreational opportunities in a truly superb natural setting. Tourist information is available from Mari Frances or Jack Greenland at the Chamber of Commerce, Box 237 Bigfork, MT 59911 or by calling 837-5888 9 to 5 Mon-Fri and 10-2 Sat. The chamber office is located just off HWY 35 in the Lakehills Shopping Center.

WHERE TO EAT

Big Fork Inn at Grand and Electric Avenue is open to serve you after 5:30 p.m. Owners Bob and Suzie Keenan provide a warm, inviting ambiance and excellent food with dancing Friday and Saturday nights. A great selection is Salmon wrapped in paper—superb! If you see Suzie be sure to ask her for a tale or two about Paris. Call 837-6680 for reservations.

Showthyme at 548 Electric Ave., phone 837-0707, is open for lunch and dinner seven days a week and is located downtown in an old bank building next to the Playhouse. Owners Rose and Blue Funk offer outstanding gourmeι food with alfresco dining in summer. Count on the cold duck salad (a great choice) or choose any of Blue's very creative and unique dishes. If you get a chance, ask Blue how Montana compares to Colorado.

Bridge Street Gallery (Don't let the name fool you!) is located where Bridge Street intersects Electric Avenue and is owned by gourmet cooks who love to share great food with guests from all over the world. Dining can be an event at this outstanding restaurant.

Picnic at Sliter's Park at the end of

Electric Avenue on the river just after you cross old iron bridge. After eating in the peaceful glen you can walk the whole town easily.

Senior Citizens' Center is located in back of the school on Commerce St. and offers lunch M-W-F at noon. Visitors are welcome but the club would appreciate a call a day in advance. Card parties twice monthly with a potluck meeting 3rd Tuesday at noon. Use of the facility for special events is invited.

"Salmon Wrapped in Paper — Superb!"

Big Fork Inn

WHERE TO STAY

Marina Cay Resort is an excellent facility with 94 units. It's located near Bigfork Harbor at 180 Vista Lane, within walking distance of many attractions. Resort has hot tub, fine restaurant, boating, Champs Sports Bar, dancing and great convention facilities. Phone 837-5861 for reservations.

O'Duachain Country Inn is a great bed-and-breakfast with five rooms at 675 Ferndale Drive, 837-6851. Owners Margot and Tom Doohan operate this rustic inn located on the outer edge of Bigfork. Margot makes the most splendid breakfasts in the Flathead Valley. You'll love the stay and great stories Tom will share about New York.

Timbers Motel and RV Park is a 40 unit classic motel on Highway 35 and within easy walking distance from downtown, phone 837-6200. Rates start at $44 for a room and facility offers 34 RV/tent sites with showers and phone. Owner Steve Blair keeps the operation in great shape but can complain occasionally about his lack of spare time.

SHOPPING

Electric Avenue Gifts at 469 Electric Ave., phone 837-3300 opens at 10 a.m. daily and offers a great selection of unique gifts, toys, cards and Made in Montana items. Laura Meissenburg is a great conversationalist and always willing to talk about Europe.

Applause at 405 Bridge St. in the heart of Bigfork. Owner Cathie Deegan offers exciting ladies' ready-to-wear.

Forget-Me-Not-Gifts, 570 Electric Ave., is owned by Luanne Van Artsdale and offers many one-of-a-kind, made in Montana gifts. If you run into Luanne, ask her about the great boating in Glacier Park.

Electric Avenue Books is owned and operated by Trish Tavenner and offers a startling variety of books and enchanting collectables. Be sure to take a peek at the wonderful grand piano in the back room and ask Trish for a run down on a few of the famous hands that have played it. Call 837-6072 for hours and information.

Bay Books and Prints is owned by bookophile and member of old Montana family, O'Neil Jones, who specializes in Montana history and art books, especially rare and out of print selections. Phone is 837-4646.

WATERING HOLES

Garden Bar at 451 Electric Ave., a popular hangout for locals, has great sandwiches and is a good spot to eat outdoors. Opens at 11 a.m. and is owned by Mark Langlois and Tom Hilley.

Chumley's Double Eagle Bar on Electric Avenue is owned by Jackie Trombly and is a great adult bar with a little bit of 30's, 40's and 50's!

The Harbor is located downtown on Grand Avenue and owned by two food and drink specialists who's idea of a good time is to make sure patrons have one. Wonderful specials and a great atmosphere.

EXHIBITS

Bigfork Art and Cultural Center at 451 Electric Ave, phone 837-6927, is managed by Joe Barnes and offers ongoing exhibitions by local artists/craftspeople. If you're in town for awhile you'll enjoy the book discussion series also.

Take a minute and stroll down Electric Avenue where you'll find eight fine galleries offering exceptional art displayed in beautiful surroundings. Only the Janoff Gallery featuring aviaton art is located off Electric on Grand Avenue. A truly wonderful way to spend an afternoon in a most hospitable community.

HISTORIC PLACES

The "Steps" can be found at the north end of Electric Avenue in downtown Bigfork and provide access to the school parking area and the upper bench above the Village. These unique stone steps were installed in the 30's by President Roosevelt's WPA after a severe flood washed out the hill section of the street.

Pacific Power and Light Bigfork Power House is located across from the old iron bridge. Construction of the powerhouse in 1901-02 provided the catalyst for the early Bigfork Village development and still supplies all the area's electrical needs.

RECREATION

Eagle Bend Golf Course at 279 Eagle Bend Drive was named the #2 new public golf course in the United States by

Golf Digest Magazine in 1989. Voted Montana's top course in 1991, this exceptional facility can be played by calling Bob Veroulis, Head Pro at 837-5615.

> **"Voted Montana's Top Course in 1991"**
>
> **Eagle Bend Golf Course**

Northshore Bowling Center at 116 Holt Drive, phone 837-5381, offers bowling 9 a.m.-11 p.m., bar noon to closing and food from 6:30 a.m. One of the best breakfasts in the valley. Contact Tim Guenzler for more information.

Nature Trail east of the Swan River Dam offers exceptional bird watching and features a pair of ospreys who have nested by the bridge for several years. Ask anyone downtown for directions, but don't bring your car, this trail is for non-motorized traffic!

Riverbend Concert Association puts on very professional performances every year from mid June to late August. Concerts are performed on the lovely Riverbend Stage at Sliter Park every Sunday night at 8:00 and music ranges from great chamber selections to Sousa Marches. For a great evening, bring a lawn chair or a blanket and be prepared to pay $3 for adults and $1 for kids.

SPECIAL EVENTS

Whitewater Festival is a great time and offers kayaking, triathalon and many other events. Kayak races are held every summer on the famous class V "Mad Mile," ending at the old iron bridge in downtown Bigfork. Call Tom Hilley at 837-9914 for more information.

Festival of the Arts comes to downtown Bigfork every July and offers two wonderful days of art and food on Main Street. Contact Sheryl Drewry at 837-4885 for details.

Christmas in Bigfork begins when the elves decorate downtown the Saturday after Thanksgiving. A Merry Christmas atmosphere prevails for the holiday season with sleigh rides, Santa Claus and more. Discover more about the magic by calling Jack Greenland at 837-5888.

EMERGENCY INFORMATION

Penco Power Products, 8537 Highway 35, phone 837-5146 is a dependable place for auto or RV repair. Mechanics' hours are 8-5 Mon-Fri. Be sure to ask owner Jeff Penrod for a story or two about the winter of '92. Towing is available from Ron Linnell at 837-2222.

Kalispell Regional Hospital is located at

310 Sunnyview Lane in Kalispell, phone 752-5111. Local 24 hour emergency medical service available by calling 911.

If your pet is in trouble, the Northshore Animal Clinic at 7575 Highway 35 can give reliable help . Call 837-6250 for an appointment or emergency help. Hours: 8:30 to 6:00 Monday-Tuesday-Wednesday and Friday: 8:30 till noon on Saturday.

BIG TIMBER

Big Timber is a great place to linger in some of Montana's best cattle country. The community is located on I-90 as it weaves through the beautiful hills and valleys of southcentral Montana. The Lewis and Clark Expedition passed through this area in 1806 and Captain William Clark named the camp "Big Timbers" because of the unusually large cottonwood trees that line the banks of the Yellowstone. For over 100 years Big Timber has been home to one of the largest Norwegian settlement in Montana, and their influence is visible today in local crafts sold at the flower shop, signs about town and the Sons of Norway events. The natives are cattlemen and sheepherders, hunters, guides, storekeepers and yarn-spinners. Many artists, poets, sculptors and history buffs now live in this inviting community and you're even likely to meet an occasional movie or television star as the Boulder Valley has become a second home to many Hollywood personalities who seem to want to experience the great outdoors in their own backyard. Tourist information is available at the Sweet Grass Chamber Visitors Center at 219 McLeod St. 9-5 Monday-Friday, at Frye's Cafe or the Victorian Village Museum. Contact Holly Wagenaar at 932-5131 for more details.

WHERE TO EAT

The Grand Hotel and Restaurant at 139 McLeod is a genuine four-star dining experience with lunch 11-3 Tuesday-Saturday, dinner 5-10 Tuesday-Sunday and Sunday Brunch 10-2. The Grand was established in 1890 and has been restored with vintage furniture in the comfortable hotel rooms. Food is prepared by chefs who know how to cook everything from Montana beef to imported seafoods. Locals like to order prime rib with all the trimmings and

"Outstanding Rack of Lamb"

The Grand Hotel

the rack of lamb (carved at tableside) with sumptuous salad is outstanding. Owners are Penelope Wilson and daughter Suzanne Wilson, manager is Larry Edwards. For reservations call 932-4459.

Frye's Cafe on Highway 10 West is owned and operated by the Snodgrass family (Jim, Lou, Craig and Diane). A landmark in Big Timber for 40 years and a favorite among locals, the rustic log building has a charming dining room with large stone fireplace and antique oak tables. The service is friendly, the food plentiful and the prices right. You won't miss with chicken fried steak or southern fried chicken dinners with salad, potatoes, vegetable, roll and dessert.

Road Kill Cafe—See Bars and Casinos

Lion's Club Park at the end of McLeod street is an ideal spot if you're pulling off the interstate for a leg stretch and or looking for a great place to picnic. There are lots of shade trees, picnic tables and even a horseshoe game if you're inclined. If you're up for a beautiful little drive, head south on 298 up the Boulder River where you'll find parks and rest areas right along the river ideal for dipping a toe or soaking up the sun atop a boulder.

WATERING HOLES

The Grand at 139 McLeod has the original back bar, bar and tile floor. Now open Tuesday through Sunday for many years it was the meeting place for card players and cowboys heading in from the ranches for the weekend after a payday. Today the cowboys mingle with shopkeepers, visitors, occasional movie stars—and the ever-amiable Norwegian-Americans out for a social hour.

McLeod Bar and Road Kill Cafe is owned by Bob and Claire Bryan and located in McLeod, 16 miles up the Boulder River on paved Highway 298. Open daily, the bar is the hub of entertainment for the beautiful valley south of Big Timber. You'll enjoy the rustic 30's atmosphere, fun folks and great sandwiches. Be sure to buy a Road Kill Cafe T-shirt; it will get comments wherever you go. (For the uninitiated, the term 'road kill' refers to animals killed by vehicles on the roadway).

The Timber Bar at 116 McLeod is open daily and run by the Fullers. The bar has been around 'pertnear' as long as Big Timber and is a favorite watering hole for all kinds of folks around the county .....as well as those passing through town. It's been refurbished and not only serves up some of the best chicken in the country, but healthy drinks by anyone's standards.

EXHIBITS

The Victorian Village Museum at exit 367 is owned and operated by Marilyn Grosfield and open 9-5 weekdays and 10-4 weekends May through September (call 932-4378 for more information). The private collection is presented in a Victorian setting, featuring a complete home from the turn-of-the-century, with charming rooms set up as they were back in Montana's early days. Each summer a special display features artifacts and antiques from local folks—

> **"Complete Home From The Turn Of The Century"**
>
> **Victorian Village Museum**

wedding gowns, toys, hats, etc. The Village side offers visitors a look at a general store, harness shop, carpenter's shop, doctor's office, dress shop, schoolhouse and one of the few remaining antique print shops in America. A real must-see on your stop in Big Timber. The antique shop offers quality items for sale at reasonable prices. If you run into Marilyn, ask her how the heck her dad managed to collect all that stuff.

Crazy Mountain Museum at exit 367 is operated by the Sweet Grass Museum Society. Open Wednesdays through Saturdays, June 1st through Labor Day. The new museum features a "Walk in Time" exhibit of archaeological finds from the area along with the Young Montana Artists and Montana Reflections exhibits and the very popular Cobblestone City miniature of 1880's Big Timber done by Orvin Fjare and Bev Josephson.

WHERE TO STAY

The Grand Hotel at 139 McLeod in downtown Big Timber is a hotel and bed-and-breakfast with 12 rooms owned by Penelope and Suzanne Wilson and managed by Larry Edwards. A main street gathering place for over 100 years, many a cattle deal was cinched at the bar and many a sheepherder hired after stepping off the train. Today it's still the place to sit down and talk shop or just have lunch. The Grand does an excellent job, whether catering to locals seeking a nice atmosphere for entertaining, or to summer visitors who delight in an overnight stay in a Victorian-style bed followed by an outstanding breakfast. It's the cornerstone of downtown Big Timber and sure to please. Call 932-4459 for reservations.

C.M. Russell Lodge on Highway 10 West has 42 units and is run by the Snodgrass family. An ideal stopping place for the traveler who wants modern comfort, good meals and a great view of the Crazy Mountains, the lodge offers a gift shop, information racks, laundry facilities and a quiet bar to enjoy a cool one after a good hunt or fantastic fishing day on the river.

A number of Sweet Grass County guest ranches offer rustic cabins at the foot of the Crazy Mountains or up the Boulder Country. Contact the Chamber at 932-

5131 or drop by the Visitor's Center to pick up a brochure for choices available if you're looking for a real change of pace and a first class country experience. Clean, attractive well furnished cabins dot the mountainsides both north and south of town.

SHOPPING

Solbergs Department Store at 108 McLeod, on the first block of main street, is reportedly the oldest department store in the state. Today it offers a complete line of men's and women's wear. Run by Bernie and Debbie Hedrick, open 8:30 to 5:30 Monday-Saturday. The Solbergs established the store in 1889 as a harness shop. A must stop for the Big Timber visitor.

Big Timber has five antique shops offering everything from western memorabilia to Victorian lace, country collectibles to glassware, linens to books. You'll definitely find something to take home. All are clean and well stocked.

Zemsky/Hines Art Gallery at 108 East 3rd Ave, phone 932-5307 is open 9-5 every day except Sunday. Located in a two-story building, it showcases the work of Jessica Zemsky and Jack Hines, both renowned artists in the area, along with paintings, sculptures and tiles of other local artists. Jack and Jessica host art workshops up the Boulder River during the summer to assist professional and amateur artists in their wildlife, scenery and portrait work. A wonderful gallery you will surely enjoy.

HISTORIC PLACES

Natural Bridge State Park is located 25 miles south of Big Timber on Highway 298. A natural wonder flowing down the Boulder Valley, this 100 foot waterfall is best viewed May through early July when the waters are at their highest. Viewers can hike a short paved trail with scenic overlooks and interpretive signs. You will enjoy taking marvelous pictures of the falls and the gorge below against the beautiful mountain backdrop. Restrooms are available.

Prairie Dog Town is found nine miles east of town on I-90. You'll be facinated as the native animals pop their heads out of their elaborate community of tunnels and holes. On warm sunny days, they are often standing upright, chirping and scampering about for food or playing rough and tumble for your viewing delight. An interpretive center describes life in a "dogtown." $3 entrance fee for vehicles May 1st through September 30th. Bring your camera to this one.

RECREATION

The Overland Golf Course is just off exit 370 and 1.1 miles east of town. The great nine-hole course designed by Max Mueller of Twin Falls, Idaho is one of the longest in the state and offers grass greens and wide, well-kept fairways. Brush makes the course very interesting and encourages accuracy. Call 932-4297 for a tee time and cart reservation.

Big Timber Waterslide is located eight miles east of town on I-90, phone 932-6570, and a great place for family fun. Three slides, two tube pools, water boats, train rides, concessions, game room, picnic area and viewing stands. Nice facility kept in top-notch shape by Ellis and May Faw. Open Memorial Day to Labor Day.

SPECIAL EVENTS

Big Timber Rodeo at the Sweet Grass Fair Grounds is one of the oldest and most exciting in the area. Held at the end of June, the NRA-sanctioned rodeo is a great favorite of locals and visitors. Call the chamber for more details.

The Pack Horse Race is truly one of a kind and hard to beat for excitement. Men's and women's teams compete for prizes and a calcutta is held the night before where visitors and participants can buy their favorite team. Contestants "pack up" and lead their pack horse on a course in rough mountain terrain. It's a major task but carried out with delight each year. Check at the McLeod Bar for directions or call 932-6174 for details and dates.

"One of a Kind Pack Horse Race"

Check at McLeod Bar

The Cutting Horse Event takes place at the end of July each year at the Fairgrounds. It's a first-class event and only part of the circuit these elegant horses and talented riders take each summer. Coming from as far away as Texas and California, riders vie for cash prizes and the competition is fierce. Watching some of the best trained horses in America cut cattle from a herd is really something, even for the novice. Phone Mary Hathaway at 932-5996.

EMERGENCY INFORMATION

Jerry's Conoco Service or Oie Motors are sure bets for honest, experienced mechanical help for your car or RV. Contact Jerry Hauge at 932-5183 or Steve Johnson at Oie's for quality service.

The Sweet Grass Community Clinic and Hospital at 5th and Hooper is available to help with medical problems. Hospital has emergency room service; phone 932-5917 and clinic is open 9-5 (phone is 932-5920). Dental help can be found by calling 932-5919.

Your pet can get help at the Big Timber Veterinary Clinic or All Creatures Veterinary Service. Call 932-5205 for Dr. Langford at the BTVC or 932-4324 for Dr. Jim Felton at the All Creatures Clinic located at Exit 370. Both should be able to give expert help from 8-5.

BRIDGER

Bridger is a rural community located thirty miles south of Laurel in the beautiful Clark's Fork Valley. The area is best know for its farm economy but also supports a variety of small businesses, including a furniture manufacturer and a computer software firm. Visitors can enjoy a wide range of recreational activities, ranging from fishing to prowling the Pryor Mountains in search of prehistoric arrowheads or fossils. Although it's less than an hour's drive to Red Lodge, Cody, the Big Horn Recreation Area or Billings, Bridger offers a quiet relaxing time among friendly folks. Tourist information is available from Betty Little at 125 South Main 8-5 or 662-3334. Betty owns Little's Real Estate, knows the territory and who to contact for more information.

WHERE TO EAT OR HAVE A DRINK

Bridger Cafe and Casino on Main St. has a comfortable, hometown atmosphere and is operated by Jack and Sue Bothman. Families are welcome and specialties include sourdough pancakes and the Sunday Smorgy. Locals particularly like the homemade pies and chicken fried steak. If you see Judy ask her about the hot Bingo games on Friday nights.

Stringtown Saloon and Eatery at 219 S. Main is a unique local pub and owner/operator Jungle Jayne serves up outstanding homemade soups and great steaks. Food is served nightly till midnight with ice cold beer available anytime. Locals like to order Jayne's Jungle Burger with a steaming bowl of cream of broccoli soup. You won't be disappointed with the hand carved finger steaks and if you get to meet Jayne, don't ask her about her latest husband.

"Jungle Jayne Serves Up Great Soups"

Stringtown Saloon & Eatery

Trapper Cafe offers good Mexican food and great breakfasts. If you see owner Polo, be sure to ask about the fishing. He can't get enough of it since moving to Montana.

Buckeye Bar and Grill at 121 N. Main has great food, honest drinks and occasional live music. Bill and Trish Asbury own and operate this rustic bar with good food at great prices. The famous Buckeye Burger is 1/2 pound of lean Montana beef on a homemade bun with fries and all the trimmin's. Other popular selections include jumbo prawns or a 16 oz. T-Bone steak dinner for $6.95.

Golden Age Society meets at the Bridger Senior Citizens' Center and offer meals on Tuesdays and Thursdays at noon. Located on east Broadway, the building is the original Northern Pacific Depot, built at the turn-of-the-century. Visitors can expect a warm welcome from president Bert Ottolino.

EXHIBITS

Clark's Fork Valley Museum at 101 East River St. just off Highway 310 in the town of Fromberg, 10 miles north of Bridger on 310, is open Father's Day till Labor Day from 11-4 daily. Violet Papp or Joan Anderson can be contacted for more information. Located in the former Northern Pacific Railroad depot, the museum opened in 1991 and offers interesting fare.

Bridger Plant Materials Center, three miles southeast of town, is open 8-5 Mon.-Fri. Managers John Scheetz and Mark Majerus run center where the U.S. Dept. of Agriculture evaluates and tests native grasses, legumes, shrubs and trees. One of twenty such facilities across the U.S., a good time to see the most varieties is late June and early July. There is an indoor display also.

Montana State Bluewater Fish Hatchery is located about five miles east of Fromberg on a gravel road. Contact Gary Shaver at 668-7682 for more information.

Plenty Coups State Park and Museum is located in Pryor, about 15 miles east of Edgar and is home of Plenty Coups, last chief of the Crow Indians. His two-story home and store remain as evidence of the Chief's efforts to lead his people in adopting the lifestyles of the white man. The museum is open for day use only. Phone Rich Pittsley at 252-1289 for more information.

Pryor Mountain Wild Horse Range is located on the Montana-Wyoming border, northwest of the boat ramp area at

> **"One of Three Wild Horse Ranges in the U.S."**
>
> **Pryor Mountain Horse Range**

Horseshoe Bend on the Bighorn Lake Reservoir. It is only one of three federally designated wild horse ranges in the United States. A sign on the right about a mile north of Horseshoe Bend marks the beginning of the range. Drive slowly, be watching and you will often see the horses, sometimes close enough to photograph. More information is available through the Bureau of Land Management Office at 222 N. 32nd St., P.O. Box 36800, Billings, MT 59107 or by calling 406-255-2925.

WHERE TO STAY

Circle of Friends Bed and Breakfast is located across from the state rest area north of town and offers three rooms,

"Comfortable Accommodations With A Western Atmosphere"

Circle of Friends Bed & Breakfast

one with private bath, in a comfortable family home with western atmosphere. Continental breakfast with homemade pastries are served and horse boarding is available. Call 622-3264 for information or brochure.

Bridger Motel at 120 N. Main is the only motel in Bridger, offers reasonable rates and is close to restaurants. Seven-unit motel is owned and operated by Bob and Linda Smith, phone 662-3212.

Campground Park on East Broadway is open May-Sept. and is the only park in Bridger that allows overnight camping. Fee is $10 nightly with park information posted on the bulletin board.

SHOPPING

Jim Bridger Trading Post at 117 S. Main offers a unique display of handcrafted, historically accurate native American reproductions. Home of the Original Montana Bean Spoon, you'll find wild rice, blankets, and a wide assortment of western items. Dealers are welcome to the shop that claims to be home of the "Greatest Traders in the Rocky Mountains". Owners Marv DeNio and Lisa Linneweh will make you feel welcome, and if you see Marv, ask about his '51 International Truck named Sanford.

The Record is the local newspaper office where you'll find reading material ranging from best-sellers for adults to coloring books for kids. Owner Shirley Randalls says travelers especially like her North American Wildlife and Charlie Russell calendars. Open 8-5 Mon.-Fri. at 123 S. Main.

Bridger True Value Hardware and Variety Store at 109 S. Main is a good source for sporting goods and local information. Owner Terry Dravetsky is usually around 8-5 Mon.-Sat. and 12-5 Sun., and can give you help with where to go and what you'll need for what ever activity interests you. Be sure to drop in and check out the buffalo and deer mounts. If you see Terry, ask about the story behind them.....it's quite a tale!

Valley Floral and Gifts at 118 S. Main has a good selection of fabrics and crafts. Store hours are 9:30-5:30 Mon.-Sat., and owner Sandy Shaver has nice display of local artwork, Graytak Prints and Montana-made gifts.

HISTORIC PLACES

The Nez Perce or Chief Joseph Trail goes through the valley and follows the route Chief Joseph and his people took from Yellowstone Park down the Clark's Fork River when pursued by the US Army in 1877. More details are available from Shirley Randalls at the Record Newspaper Office.

"Bozeman Trail Historic Marker"

Highway 212

The Bozeman Trail is marked by an Historic marker on Highway 212 in Joliet just north of Bridger. In the 1860's, John Bozeman, young adventurer, and Jim Bridger, grand old man of the mountains, guided rival wagon trains of emigrants and gold-seekers through the area over routes variously called Bonanza Trail, Bridger Cut-off or Bozeman Road from Fort Laramie Wyoming to Virginia City, Montana. The trail crossed Indian country in direct violation of treaty and was a "cut off" used by impatient pioneers who considered the time saved worth the danger.

Jim Bridger, Mountain Man Highway Sign located on the south edge of Bridger on Highway 310 recounts Jim Bridger's arrival in Montana in 1822 as a member of a Rocky Mountain Fur Company brigade. For years, he had no more permanent home than a poker chip meandering the entire Rocky Mountain region and often coming through this part of the country. A keen observer and a natural geographer with years of experience amongst the Indians, he became invaluable as a guide and scout for wagon trains and federal troops following the opening of the Oregon Trail. He shares honors with John Colter for first discoveries in the Yellowstone Park country. Prone to elaborate a trifle for the benefit of pilgrims, it was Jim who embroidered his story of the petrified forest by asserting that he had seen a petrified bird sitting in a petrified tree singing a petrified song. The Clark's Fork of the Yellowstone that runs through Bridger was named for Captain William Clark of the Lewis and Clark Expedition in 1804-1806.

The Pryor Mountains are located east of Bridger and cover about 300,000 acres, once entirely Crow Indian Territory. The mountains came by their name indirectly from Pryor Creek, which Captain William Clark named for expedition member Sergeant Nathaniel Pryor. The mountains hold many intriguing discoveries, including ice caves, sinks, caverns and such archaeological finds as Clovis points that document human occupation there as long as 10,000 years ago. South of the

> **"Look For Clovis Points That Document Human Occupation 10,000 Years Ago"**
>
> **Pryor Mountains**

range, the remains of log and frame houses and barns attest to the homesteads staked after passage of the Forest Homestead Act of 1906. Though they cultivated some crops, for many homesteading was a pretense for mountain grazing on adjacent forest and reservation ranges. For more information about area pictographs and pectroglyphs, ancient caves and campsites, frontier trails, railroad traces or weather-worn cabins and homesteads, contact the Bureau of Land Management Office at 222 N. 32nd St., Billings, MT, write to Box 36800, Billings, MT 59107 or phone 406-255-2913.

Pryor Mountain Road can be reached by turning east off Highway 310 2 miles south of Bridger. Sagecreek Campground at elevation 5600' is 22 miles east and has 12 primitive camp spaces. The Big Ice Cave has a day use picnic area and you'll find several undeveloped caves in the area. The Dryhead Overlook is near the Big Ice Cave and offers a view few will forget. Four wheel drive vehicles are not necessary but use caution as wet weather can make local clay soils treacherous.

Walking Tour of Historic Buildings in Bridger is a great opportunity to view 14 homes and commercial buildings around town listed on the National Register of Historic Places. A brief description of each along with a location on a self-guided tour map is available at the Bridger Town Hall or Little's Real Estate office.

RECREATION SPECIAL EVENTS

Bridger Rodeo activities are held at the Rodeo Grounds SW of town adjacent to the airport. Contact Glen or Viki Booke at 662-3216 for information on what's happening. Rex Kock, at 662-3216 is an active member of the local roping club and a good source of information about these interesting events. Team roping is held each year in May, August and Sept. on Tue., Fri. and Sun. evenings. Viewing is free and non-members can rope for $10 a night. Jim Bridger Days PRCA Rodeo is a very special event held the third weekend in July each year. You won't be disappointed with this local rodeo as the Bridger facility was honored in 1991 as having the best small rodeo grounds in Montana and the affair was singled out as one of the top 20 local rodeos in the country by the Western Heritage Museum in Portland, Oregon. Routinely eight to 10 participants make it to the national finals in the Youth Rodeo Division, no small accomplishment considering the small community event.

"Viewing is Free And Non-Members Can Rope For $10 Per Night"

Team Roping

Jim Bridger Park at the south end of town on Highway 310 is a good spot to picnic with off road parking. Created by the Local Lions Club in 1976, it marks a historic river crossing site of Jim Bridger.

EMERGENCY INFORMATION

You can trust your vehicle to Bridger Conoco at 312 N. Main. Owner/operator Roger Teesdale can be reached at 662-3633 and a mechanic is on duty 7-6 Mon.-Sat.

Clark's Fork Medical Center at 410 S. 2nd St. in Bridger is open 8:30-12 and 1-5 Mon.-Tue.-Thur.-Fri. and 8:30-12 on Sat. Phone 662-3566 or 662-3627. Ambulance can be reached at 662-3333 and the clinic does have a fully equipped emergency room. Certified Physician Assistant and Registered Nurse on duty.

If your pet needs help the Bridger Vet. Clinic east of town can help with DVS Ray Randall available 8-5 Mon-Sat at 662-3330. The clinic does have mobile services and boarding is available.

CASCADE

Cascade is a community of about 800 located on the banks of the Missouri River. Farming and ranching provide the economic base for the town located 25 miles south of Great Falls on I-15 in the heart of some great hunting and fishing country in and around the Smith River and Holter Lake. Famous Montana artist Charlie Russell lived and painted in the Cascade area. He and his wife Nancy were married there, and the home they lived in still stands today. Tourist Information is available at the City Hall or the Wedsworth Library. City Hall hours are 9-5 Mon.-Fri. and library is open 10-12 summers and 3-5 winters. Contact Barbara Hitt, Clerk or Librarian Jackie Strandell at 468-2808.

WHERE TO EAT

Badger Cafe at 132 1st. St. is managed by Dayna Edwards and open 7 a.m. to 8 p.m. daily. You won't be disappointed if you try the mushroom burger, club sandwich or cinnamon rolls in this clean, friendly cafe.

Missouri River Inn, nine miles south of Cascade at 2427 Old Highway 91, is open 6 a.m. to 10 p.m. and is run by owners Bud and Joan Osterman. The food is great and there's likely to be dancing on weekends. Sure bets are chicken dinners, steaks and hamburgers. Call 468-9884 for more information.

> **"Sure Bets Are Chicken Dinners, Steaks And Burgers"**
>
> **Missouri River Inn**

WHERE TO STAY

A & C Motel at 308 1st Ave. is very clean and reasonably priced.

Owner/manager of the operation is Alice Cobb, phone 468-2513.

Badger Motel at 132 First Street North is brand new and owned by Terry and Pam Curnow, phone 468-9330.

SHOPPING

Kitson's at 100 N. 1st offers nice selection of clothing for the whole family along with boots, T shirts and jewelry.

WATERING HOLES

Driftwood Bar and Grill at 9 Central Ave is open 10 a.m. to 2 a.m., run by owners Roger, Jackie and Joel Strandell and serves great burgers and fries.

Sportsman's Club Bar at 12 Central, is operated by Dennis Hall and open 11 a.m. to 2 a.m.

Angus Bar and Cafe at 20 Central is owned by Kate Stoner and Marvin Marten, serves great food and is open 7-8.

EXHIBITS

Cascade Historical Museum located at 101 Front Street is open 10-5 Mon.-Fri. Good selection of items of interest from the surrounding area.

"Mission Was Started In About 1860 And the Church Is Still Available For Viewing"

St. Peters Mission

St. Peters Mission is located 19 miles NW of town on the frontage road. Originally planned as a school for the Blackfeet Indians, the mission was started in about 1860 and the church is still available for viewing. History of the facility is provided in book "The Bird Tail" by Sister Genevieve McBride.

HISTORIC PLACES

Ulm Pishkun Buffalo Jump is located 14 miles west of Great Falls near Ulm, Montana. Used by Indians for hunting before the horse was introduced in the late 1600's, this land was recently purchased by Ted Turner.

RECREATION

Holter Lake Lodge and Gates of the Mountains is located near Craig, Montana and open Memorial Day to Labor Day. Boat tours are available about four times daily. Call 458-5241 for schedule or more information.

Campground is available at the Atkinson Park and Swimming Pool on the west end of 3rd Avenue.

EMERGENCY INFORMATION

If you're in need of vehicle repair, you can count on Rod Thompson at Cascade Auto, 468-2234 or George Franko at the Blacksmith's Shop, 468-2553. Parts and advice easily found at Napa Store, 19 N. 1st from Don or Clara Mae Fraser, 468-9236.

Although there's no medical facility for you in town, if your pet's hurting, Bill Patton at the Indian Hammer Veterinarian Clinic is available from 8-5 at 7 S. 1st or by calling 468-2207 or 235-4359.

COLUMBUS

Located at exit 408 on I-90, Columbus is nestled in the pine covered hills along the Beartooth Range, at the junction of the beautiful Stillwater and Yellowstone rivers. Agriculture and ranching still play a very important role for this community of 1500, but the local economy is enhanced by a unique variety of industries—Montana Silversmiths, a manufacturer of buckles and other silver jewelry items that is rapidly becoming a dominant wholesaler throughout the world; Timberweld, a laminated structural wood manufacturer; Stillwater Mining Co.'s Precious Metals Smelter, the only one of its kind in the United States. With early town names like Eagle's Nest, Sheep Dip and Stillwater, Columbus is a good place to get off the interstate to start a trip to Yellowstone Park via the beautiful Highway 78 through Absarokee, Red Lodge and the breathtaking Beartooth Pass. Along the way you'll see great scenery and enjoy a panoramic view of America's only platinum/palladium mine at Nye. Tourist Information is available by contacting the Columbus Chamber of Commerce representative, Bruce Nathan at 332-5366.

WHERE TO EAT

Branding Iron Cafe at 1036 E. Pike is operated by Jean Lloyd and offers great homemade soups and desserts. Enjoy the friendly small town service with one of Jean's daily specials and stop in Saturday night for a Mexican feast.

Apple Village Cafe and Gift Shop, just off I-90, is open 24 hours a day, May-Dec., and owner Donna Godwin has great deli sandwiches and very special six inch homemade hamburger pies. Very clean cafe with pleasant atmosphere offers great family dining. Sunday Brunch is sure to please from 11-3.

Gino's Pizza Shoppe at 416 Pike is run by Gene and Margaret Schmid and puts out some of the best pizza and calzones you'll find anywhere. Locals like to order Grandma's special pizza and the homemade cheesecake. Margaret is great, Gene whistles, and if you see him ask how many screens he's given away today.

WHERE TO STAY

Columbus Super 8, just off the Interstate, is a 72-unit facility run by Michele Orlich and offers spa, sauna & fitness center, guest laundry, large vehicle parking, remote control cable, free local calls, non-smoking rooms, suites and meeting room. Fuel, snacks and a 24-hour restaurant are just next door. It's AAA approved with reservations available by calling 322-4101 or 800-442-4667.

Itch-Kep-Pe Park has 49 campsites in two locations amid 100-year-old cottonwoods. Access is from Highway 78 just north of the Yellowstone River Bridge on the way to Absarokee. Both upper and lower parks feature gravelled campsites, cooking grills, tables, benches and free firewood. The upper park has flush toilets and an open, airy setting, while the lower park offers a more solitary experience with dense natural vegetation. Although the campground is free, donations to support maintenance by the local Kiwanis Club can be made at the collection station in the upper park restroom.

"Great Campsites Surrounded By 100-Year-Old Cottonwoods"

Itch-Kep-Pe Park

SHOPPING

Bertha's is a unique small-town store at 428 Pike and open 8:30-5:30 Mon.-Fri., 8:30-5 on Sat. Owned and operated by Bertha Neville, you'll find a great selection of fashion clothing and an interesting mix of gift items.

Stillwater Hardware at 508 Pike is open 8-5:30 Mon.-Sat. and 11-4 Sun., and is run by owner Gene Orlenbush. A hometown hardware store, you'll find good stock of sporting goods and supplies as well as good advice from Gene.

Bruursema Jewelers at 508 Pike is open 9-5, owned and operated by Doug Bruursema and offers a good selection of Black Hills Gold, Montana Yogo Sapphires and Montana Silversmith Jewelry.

Organized Confusion Variety Shoppe at 30 N. 4th Street is open 10-6:30 and owned and operated by Pat Pillion and Virginia Rohrer. This new business

> **"Pat Will Hem, Mend And Install Zippers On The Spot!"**
>
> **Organized Confusion Variety Shoppe**

features Montana-made crafts, both purchased and on consignment, new and used books, clothing and videos. Pat will hem, mend and install zippers on the spot and if you see Virginia, ask her about how they named their store.

White Bird Gallery and Frame in the Apple Village Center just off the Interstate is owned and run by Walter J. Marten and open 10-6 Mon.-Sat. Great originals and prints of western and wildlife art along with a unique selection of antiques, Indian jewelry, mountain man crafts and many other interesting items. Call Walt at 322-5440 for more details.

Harvest Home is located a half a mile off the Interstate at the corner of 9th Street and 2nd Avenue and is open seven days a week. Owner Cathie Osmun has antiques, collectibles, jewelry, crafts and artwork from over 100 local craftsmen and artists on display in a homey atmosphere. If you see Cathie's husband Duane, be sure to ask him about his Rolls Kinardly parked on the lawn.

The Shed and State Liquor Store at 929 East 4th is owned by Robert Maurer. It is open from 8:30-5:30 and offers a variety of new and used merchandise on one half of the store, and liquor on the other.

Eagles Nest Floral and Gifts at 412 East Pike has a good selection of made in Montana crafts and gift items, jewelry, antiques, pottery and figurines, plus silk and dried floral arrangements, and, of course, fresh flowers and lush plants.

Stillwater Book Nook at 510 E. Pike is open 9-5:30 most days and operated by Dennis Goosey. Along with office supplies, greeting cards, western prints and scale models, you'll find all kinds of books, including those about Montana by local authors. If you see Marty, don't ask him about 4-wheeling unless you've got a lot of time on your hands.

WATERING HOLES

New Atlas Bar at 528 Pike is truly unique with a back bar you won't soon forget and one of the largest collections of animal mounts in the Northwest. Well worth the stop!

Sports Hut at 341 N. 9th is easy to find just a mile off the interstate, owned and operated by Rik and Fred and opens at 10 daily. Place has great chicken and curly fries for under $5.00, a half-pound burger that's closer to 3/4 pounds and a friendly atmosphere. If you see Fred ask him why he dresses like a sneaker salesman.

> **"Outstanding Animal Mount Collection"**
>
> New Atlas Bar

HISTORIC PLACES

Columbus Mountain View Cemetery, located just west of town on old Highway 10, is included in the National Register and has numerous ornate and historic gravestones that are facinating. Examples of the Petosa Monument Company's work found in the cemetery were exhibited at the World's Fair in St. Louis in 1904 and the Wimsett headstone, a carved tree trunk entwined with sandstone ivy, was a prize-winner there.

The Stone Quarry produced the sandstone for the state capitol building in Helena, and for 10 years at the turn of the century, a quarry crew sawed sandstone on the bluffs north of Columbus, near the present city water storage tank. Local evidence of the quarry's heyday exists in Columbus, one being Quarry Street, originally the route of a railroad spur used for stone transport. Products of the quarry include the Mike Jacobs home at the corner of Quarry and First Avenue North. Quarry owner Mike Jacobs' imposing stone residence is a local monument to the Columbus Quarry. The little Stone Church stands next to the Community Congregational Church on Fourth Street and started life as Columbus' second schoolhouse. Built nearly 20 years before its impressive brick neighbor, it once boasted a bell tower used to call children to class before the turn of the century.

The Colonel Norton Home stands next to the Stillwater Courthouse at the north end of Fourth Street. Civil war veteran, William Norton, nicknamed the "Colonel," built it of locally kilned red brick. A town founder with Horace Countryman, Norton operated a store on the corner of Pike Avenue and Fifth St., now occupied by Line Western Drug. Countryman ran the famous early log hotel a block west on the corner of Pike and Fourth where a 7-Day Mart now stands and became nationally famous when a tired Muggins Taylor galloped into what is now Columbus in 1876 with the official notice of the Custer Massacre. Newspaper correspondent Norton re-wrote the message which Countryman carried to the Helena telegraph line on a fresh horse.

Museum of the Beartooths is located at the corner of 5th Street and 5th Avenue. Although a new addition to town, a significant effort is underway to develop historic displays. Contact the Chamber of Commerce for hours of operation.

RECREATION

Columbus Golf Course is located just off the road to Absarokee on 3rd Avenue South. Contact 322-4298 for a tee time on the well maintained, picturesque course near the Yellowstone River. Fly-in golfing is available as course is located within walking distance of the airport. You won't be disappointed by the condition of the course, and small greens make play challenging. Greens fees are $7 and $13 and carts may be rented for $8 or $12. Club rental is available and tee times can be scheduled anytime.

Fishing is good in this beautiful stretch where the Stillwater enters the Yellowstone. Boat ramps are available in Itch-Kep-Pe Park and you'll find the scenery as good as the fishing with the magnificent Beartooths creating a backdrop for soaring eagles, geese and ducks. Columbus is a gateway to numerous forest accesses into the heart of the Absaroka-Beartooth Wilderness and its unmatched, high alpine lake fishing.

EMERGENCY INFORMATION

Bob Kem's Auto Repair at 36 Pike can be counted on for fast, fair repair 8-5 Mon.-Fri. and 8-12 Sat. Reach owner/operator Bob Kem at 322-5996.

Stillwater Community Hospital is available for your personal health needs 24 hours a day at 44 W. 4th Ave. North, phone 322-5316. Emergency help is available at same number.

Should your pet have a problem, the Cloverleaf Veterinary Service on the North Frontage Road in Columbus can give reliable help 9-5:30 Mon.-Fri. and 9-12 on Sat. Call 322-4581 for an appointment or in case of an emergency.

CULBERTSON

Culbertson is over 100 years old and located near the Missouri River in northeastern Montana, 22 miles from the North Dakota border and 60 miles from Canada. A small farming and ranching community with a lot to offer the visitor, Culbertson's fishing and hunting are a big favorite of locals and travelers alike. Residents are great community supporters of activities centered around church and school. A true western town offering warm western hospitality to all who visit. You are sure to be greeted with a smile and friendly hello from everyone you meet. Visitor information is available at the Culbertson Museum from 9-5 May-Sept., or by calling 787-6320.

WHERE TO EAT

M & M's Place at 14th Ave. E. and 6th St. on Highway 2 is owned and operated by Mel and Margaret Torgerson. Locals like the great hamburgers and ice cream treats.

Me Too Pizzeria at 3rd St. and 4th Ave. W. on Main St. is open 11-9, owned by Lee and Laurie Averill and managed by Ray and Jean Oelkers. You'll find the best pizza and subs in town, great daily specials, and if you see Laurie, ask her how she makes her outstanding white cheese pizza.

"Outstanding White Cheese Pizza"

Me Too Pizzeria

Wild West Diner on Highway 2 at 20th and 6th Ave. E. is operated by Bob and Marie Damm and open from 6 a.m. to 9 p.m. daily. Locals like the hearty meals, western hospitality and daily noon specials. Specialties include great hamburgers and steaks. If you run into Marie, ask her about the old railroad car.

Centennial Park and Campground on the truck route has covered picnic tables, a nice playground and free R.V. camping with hookups.

Culbertson Swimming Pool is a pleasant place to stop, take a break and watch the kids during the summer. Picnic tables and playground are available.

Culbertson Horseshoe Club on Highway 16 has picnic tables and a good chance for a game of horseshoes with a friendly local.

WHERE TO STAY

Diamond Willow Inn at junction of Highways 2 and 16 is run by Larry and Pam Damm and is a very popular place with hunters each year. Clean, cozy and located just across the street from restaurants, the motel has a book and Bible store with many unique gift ideas. Phone 787-6218 for reservations.

"Popular Place For Hunters"

Diamond Willow Inn

Kings Inn is a 20 unit AAA motel at 408 E. 6th on Hwy 2 East, phone 787-6218. Owned by Jay and Donnie King, you'll find large rooms, queen beds, HBO, air conditioning and free coffee.

Centennial Park is run by the city and located on the truck route. It's nicely shaded with a playground, free overnight spaces with hook-ups available and just 2 blocks from downtown.

SHOPPING

Culbertson Drug at 119 Broadway, phone 787-5313, is owned and operated by Arnie and Irene Johnson and open from 9-5:30 most days. Nice selection of gifts compliments the pharmacy.

Gambles at 122 Broadway, phone 787-5213, is run by Bernie and Montana Finnicum 8-5:30. Great spot to get the lowdown on local hunting and fishing and if you see Bernie, he can probably get anything you need.

The Other Place at 105 Broadway, phone 787-5211, is also owned by Bernie and Montana Finnicum and open 9-5:30. Store offers clothing for everyone and a nice selection of jewelry.

WATERING HOLES

The Coach Bar and Lounge at 602 6th Ave. E. on Hwy 2 is open at 10 daily and offers cozy atmosphere with friendly smiles, a good menu and is owned/

operated by Nancy and Brook Hjelm. If you see Nancy, be sure to ask for a taste of their famous super nachos.

Montana Bar at 23 Broadway, is open at 10 daily, has a good menu and is run by Bob Linthicum. With an Old West atmosphere, this is great gathering spot for locals and a friendly place to stop. If you get to meet Bob, he'll be happy to pass along the latest joke.

EXHIBITS

Culbertson Museum is located east of town on Hwy 2, phone 787-6320. Open May-Sept., 9-5 Mon.-Fri. and 1-5 Sundays with special evening viewing available by calling 787-5337 or 787-5515. Take a walk through yesterday and view the history of pioneer homesteads. Admission is free and the facility does have wheel chair access. For more information contact Museum President Myra Gustafson or Secretary/Treasurer Ruth Mattelin.

HISTORIC PLACES

Forts Union and Bufford are only a half-hour drive from Culbertson on the North Dakota/Montana border and offer an exceptional insight into history of the West. Located where the Yellowstone and Missouri Rivers meet, trappers and traders would bring their furs and goods to be shipped back East. Well worth your while and both are most enjoyable stops.

"Half-Hour Drive To Forts Union And Buford"

RECREATION

The Missouri River south of Culbertson is in beautiful country and offers great walleye fishing in the summer, ling fishing in the winter, and of course, unbeatable hunting each fall for visitors from all over the country.

SPECIAL EVENTS

Threshing Bee is held each fall south of town on Hwy 16. You'll find activities for young and old with two full days of yesteryear celebrations. Antique parade both days with Fiddlers' Jamboree and Bar-B-Que on Saturday. Contact Cliff Johnson at 525-3621 or Rodney Iverson at 787-5265 for details.

Culbertson Saddle Club Trail Ride is held every September and offers an exceptional experience as people from all over enjoy two days reliving the Old

West. Horseback riders, covered wagons and buggies can all be seen on the prairie. Night stop includes a great cowboy meal, a dance under the stars and outdoor camping...truly unbeatable, old-fashioned fun. Lloyd Aspenlieder can give you dates and more information at 787-5345.

"Night Stop Includes A Great Cowboy Meal And Dance Under The Stars"

Culbertson Saddle Club Trail Ride

Frontier Days in June each year offers 2 days of rootin' tootin' western fun. Parades on Saturday at 3:00 and Sunday at 12:00. The 'open' amateur Rodeo is great fun on Saturday at 6:30 and Sunday at 2:30. You'll really enjoy the Community Follies Saturday at 4 and a Street Dance Saturday night. A great local event.

River Float on the Missouri south of town is held annually, and it's a great event for all concerned. Contact Ken Forbregd at 787-5771 for dates and more information.

Roosevelt County Fair is held in August each year. Good wholesome entertainment for all, the fair offers exhibits of livestock, sewing, crafts, gardening, school activities and more. Special events include Farm Hand and Jr. Farm Hand Olympics and Make-It-and-Take-It. This fair is what county fairs should still be like everywhere.

EMERGENCY INFORMATION

Oelkers Exxon at 4 6th Ave. E. can give you reliable help for vehicle problems at a fair price. Owned and run by Ron and Gordon Oelkers, phone 787-5315, the shop is open 7 a.m. to 9 p.m. most days. You'll enjoy dealing with this family business when you're in need.

Roosevelt Memorial Hospital at 818 2nd Avenue East keeps regular clinic hours from 9-5, phone 787-6215, and 24-hour emergency care is available by calling 787-6281. Nearest fully equipped emergency room is at Mercy Hospital in Williston N.D.

Western Veterinary Clinic can be counted on to take care of your pet with T.L.C. Located in Williston at Hwy 2 and 85, you can call 1-800-828-6681 or 572-7878 for hours and directions.

CUT BANK

The city of Cutbank had its beginning soon after 1891 when the Great Northern Railway was on its westward expansion. The original townsite was on the west side of the Cut Bank River, on the Blackfeet Indian Reservation, until it was relocated on the private land on the other side in 1900. The vast area to the west became a grazing bonanza dominated by huge cattle herds, tended by cowpunchers who came to Cut Bank to get supplies, visit local saloons and socialize. Located less than 50 miles from the scenic wonders of Glacier Park, this community of over 4,000 has an economic base built on agriculture and the oil/gas industry. Tourist information is available at the Edward D. Jones and Co. offices, 21 S. Central, or by contacting Pam Smith at 873-4184.

WHERE TO EAT

Maxi's Pizza and Ribs on the east edge of town is run by Max and Zita Cebulla and offers great service and outstanding food. Locals order a lot of pizza and chicken and if you see Maxi, get him talking about Glacier Park; you'll enjoy it thoroughly.

Quarter Circle at 502 W. Main opens at 5 and has great coffee, fresh biscuits and gravy and super pie. Owner is Patti Momberg but if you see Kelly, don't hesitate to tease her a little, she's got a great disposition.

> **"Don't Hesitate To Tease Kelly"**
>
> **Quarter Circle Cafe**

Greco's at 112 N. Central is a great place to stop for coffee and fresh rolls. If Fred's around, ask him how his golf game is doing.

J.R.'s at 918 E. Main is run by Joan and a sure bet for fine dining and good drinks. Salad bar is a local favorite.

WHERE TO STAY

Northern Motor Inn at 609 W. Main, run by Lee Coe, is the newest motel in the area, phone is 873-5662. Location is convenient next to the mall and Pizza Hut.

Glacier Motor Inn is a classic motel at 15 1st Ave. S.E. with a bar and restaurant. If you get a chance to meet owner/operator Misha encourage her to talk about her homeland, it's facinating.

SHOPPING

Drug Mart in the Shopping Center is owned and operated by Ron and Cathy Campbell and open 9-9. As well as a drug store, you'll find a nice selection of gifts and books. If you meet Cathy, ask her how she's bowling.

Gooseberry Patch in the Shopping Center is run by Luana Johnson, open 10-5:30 and offers visitors an interesting selection of crafts and novelties.

WATERING HOLES

Glacier Bar is in the Glacier Motor Inn at 15 1st Avenue S.E. and is also run by Misha. You'll be pleased with friendly atmosphere and reasonable drink prices.

The Den at 3 N. Central has a rustic atmosphere and offers the best shrimp cocktails around.

"Best Shrimp Cocktails Around"

The Den

The Village in the Shopping Center has both restaurant and bar, and of course, good supply of Keno and Poker machines for your gambling pleasure.

EXHIBITS

Glacier County Historical Museum is located just off the Old Kevin Hwy just a couple miles west of town. Open 1-5 Tuesday-Saturday, you can make arrangements for viewing other times by calling Frances Lasorte at 873-4519 or Mary Jane Moore at 873-2157. Displays include a cable tool oil derrick, a schoolhouse built in 1914 and farm machinery. Museum building contains an interesting selection of clothing, pictures, toys, and features a tack room, old store and much more. Questions about local history can be directed to the Glacier County Historical Society, Box 576, Cut Bank, MT 59427.

RECREATION

Cutbank Golf and Country Club has 9 holes, grass greens and was completed in 1957. Tee times can be arranged by calling 873-2574.

Hunting, fishing, skiing and snowmobiling are all available within a few minutes of Cutbank.

SPECIAL EVENTS

Lewis and Clark Days are held annually. For information about this interesting three-day event, call Penne Swenson at 873-2589 or 873-4128.

EMERGENCY INFORMATION

You can trust your car to Mel Sinclair at Mel's, 122 E. Main, phone 873-2481. If you see Mel, ask him to brag a little about the great service Damion gives.

Glacier Memorial Hospital at 802 2nd St. S.E. is open 24 hours a day and has fully equipped emergency room. Call 873-2251 for appointment or 911 for emergency.

Northern Veterinary Clinic on Hwy 55 North can care for your pet and is open 8-6 most days. Phone 873-5604 during business hours or Dr. Gary Cassel at 873-2388 in emergency.

DILLON

Visited by the Lewis and Clark Expedition in 1805 who named Beaverhead Rock, Dillon is located in the center of Beaverhead County and in the heart of ranching country. The county is Montana's largest cattle producer and literally ranked fourth in the whole country in this industry. The town got its name from Sidney Dillon, an early day railroad president. It sprung up around 1880 as a mobile town, moving with the railroad. Even before the town was founded, gold was discovered near Bannack, a neighboring community to the west, and the area flourished. Mining is still represented by Barrett Minerals Inc., which boasts 100+ area employees. In addition, Dillon has been the home of the 22-acre campus of Western Montana College for over a century. Sharing the out of doors with mother nature in this area is truly something special. The two million acre Beaverhead National Forest has its headquarters in Dillon and the area is a hub for hunting and fishing activity from all around the country. Both the Beaverhead and Big Hole Rivers have international status as Blue Ribbon Trout streams. Tourist information is available from the Beaverhead Chamber of Commerce located downtown on S. Montana St. from 8-4:30 or by calling representative Cathy Burwell at 683-5511. A visit there will be worth your while as you'll get a look at the beautifully restored Union Pacific railroad depot with a very special room featuring a Lewis and Clark diorama with waxen figures and detailed backdrop now a designated "Entrance to Montana" and tourist information center.

WHERE TO EAT

Lion's Den Supper Club at 725 N. Montana is owned by Casey Keltz and Dick Motta and managed by Donnie Keltz. You'll like the newly remodeled and redecorated bar with a display featuring Benny Reynolds, a local cowboy who won fame as the World's Champion and who still competes on the Old Timer Circuit.....a real Montana legend. Locals like to order the Prime Rib and you'll find it's great. It includes all the extras and is usually more than you can eat. For lunch try the chicken fried steak sandwich with gravy and special

> **"Great Display Featuring Benny Reynolds"**
>
> Lion's Den Supper Club

fries. If you see Donnie ask him to explain the "Udder-Tugging Contest" they sponsor every spring.

Papa T's at 10 N. Montana is owned and operated by Tom "Papa T" Loman, his wife Evelyn and their daughter and son-in-law, Geri and Paul Godecke. Always offering great food and fast, friendly service, you won't miss with a deli sandwich and the famous cottage fries. Homemade soup is always a favorite and their pizza is a specialty.

Picnic next to the water station and falls at Barrets Station. A pretty spot away from the hustle and bustle of traffic, it's located 7 miles south of town on Hwy 91.

If a service club suits you, try the local Elks. They welcome all members with guests and have a great facility at 27 E. Center.

WHERE TO STAY

Paradise Inn at 650 N. Montana is a great place for the traveler that wants to find rest, recreation, relaxation and good food all in one location. Sixty units are complimented by a beautiful indoor pool with hot tub and exercise room. Great restaurant and lounge where you'll always be greeted with a smile and easy access off I-15. Phone is 683-4214.

Beaverhead Rock Ranch Guest House is located just 10 miles south of Dillon on Highway 91 and truly just what you've always dreamed of. A perfect getaway, yet close to town, owners Gary and Sonja Williams provide outstanding hospitality and their charming guest house offers quiet seclusion complimented by all the comforts of home. The special location has some of the best fishing and nature hikes in the area and while you're there, be sure to ask Sonja and Gary about the history of the area and Lewis and Clark's journey through it. Sonja is the curator of the local museum and has a wealth of knowledge about Beaverhead County history.

Southside RV Park at 104 E. Poindexter has 42 spaces and is owned and operated by Jim and Shirley McAndrews. Lovely, grassy sites, shade trees and a creek running through brings travelers back to stay again and again at this picturesque RV park. Services available include electricity, water/sewer hook-ups, cable TV, bathrooms, showers, laundry room, gift shop, recreation hall, horseshoe pits and picnic tables. Seems like everything you could be looking for! Shirley will be happy to tell you about the historic walking tour in Dillon and points of interest in the area. She's a wealth of information and knows just what you would like to see in beautiful Beaverhead country.

> **"Lovely, Grassy Sites With Shade Trees And A Creek"**
>
> **Southside RV Park**

SHOPPING

3-D (Dillon Discount Depot) at 130 S. Montana is owned and operated by Leta Grogan. Open most days 8-5:30, it's jam-packed with clothing and gifts. They feature many Montana-made items and "you design" T-shirts. Great place to stop and get something to take home to a friend or relative. Easy to find directly across from the new visitor's center.

Gracie's Second Hand and Antique Store is open 8-5 and located at 140 W. Bannack. A one-of-a-kind place, you'll find the unique rock and glass fence and totem pole very interesting. The owners say if you can't find what you want, you just haven't looked hard enough! This is one place you won't want to miss. When you meet Gracie, ask her about "Logan's Lake," her beautiful private oasis along I-15.

Thomas Company Jewelers at 37 S. Idaho is owned by Tom Keith and features a large inventory of traditional diamond and precious stone jewelry with an excellent selection of quality watches. The most unique feature of the store is the exceptional Elk Ivory jewelry custom designed and crafted by Tom. Very popular with hunters and anyone with an eye for the unusual. Traditional casting and custom jewelry design are also available from this wonderful craftsman.

WATERING HOLES

The Mine Shaft at 26 S. Montana is one of the newer lounges in Dillon and is owned by Fred Throckmorton. It's located in the historic O.E. Morse building across from the Beaverhead Museum where you'll enjoy a relaxed atmosphere in a very posh, yet rustic setting. Mining tools and antiques are on display and a great selection of steaks offered on the excellent menu. Fred is very knowledgeable and is always willing to share the history of the area, the building and his very interesting antiques.

The Metlen Hotel Bar and Cafe at 5 S. Railroad is owned by Sandy Alley and is an interesting stop. The historic hotel dates back to 1897 as the stone used for a part of the structure came from the quarries near Dillon. Be sure to check out the beautiful backbar, and if the mood strikes you, enjoy the live music and large dance floor that's hopping most weekends. Breakfasts are truly wonderful with lots of good old-fashioned pancakes, eggs or whatever suits you.

"Wonderful Breakfasts"

Metlen Hotel Cafe

Lion's Den (See Restaurants) is a popular watering hole in Dillon and located just off the Interstate where the unique bar has silver dollars set into it. Donnie serves up some of the best mixed drinks in town and always has your brand of beer on hand. Occasional live music.

EXHIBITS

Beaverhead County Museum is located at 15 South Montana. Curator Sonia Williams has assembled a large inventory of local and Montana artifacts. You'll be fascinated by the small original cabin furnished with pioneer furniture and fixtures, many pieces of mining equipment and a special section dedicated to Bannack. Other displays include furnishing and clothing of the settlers and pioneers of Beaverhead County, rocks and gemstones found within the county, and a large mounted Kodiak bear greets you as you enter. The museum is easily worth an hour or two of browsing and Sonia can be contacted at 683-5027 for tours if you'd like a real personal touch. The "Entrance to Montana" Visitor Information Center in the Union Pacific Depot Building at 125 S. Montana Street has been restored to its historic elegance and is a must for visitors to Dillon. The main attraction is the Lewis and Clark diorama in the north room with original oak bench and baggage cart. Also featured is an excellent "Mammoth Digs" prehistoric display. The south end of the Center houses the summer theater with plush seats and weekly presentations from the Shortline Players between July 9th and Labor Day, Thur.-Sat. nights. Phone the Visitor's Center at 683-5511 for more information.

Western Montana College Gallery and Museum is located at 710 S. Atlantic and open Monday-Friday from 1-5 and 7-9. Curator Sylvia Kimzey offers travel exhibits, student art, and the spectacular Seidensticker Wildlife Collection of Asian, African and North American trophies. You really must see to appreciate.

HISTORIC PLACES

Bannack was the first Territorial Capital of Montana and is an historically restored ghost town located just four miles off Hwy 41 West and 20 miles SW of Dillon. Queen of the gold camps and home of the famous Vigilantes who put an end to the raids of Montana's notorious Sheriff Plummer and his gang, Bannack is now preserved as one of the jewels of the Montana State Park system. Its sixty buildings and hundreds of artifacts displayed in a realistic setting are truly a must if you're at all interested in western history. Be prepared for a $3 per vehicle State Park fee.

> **"Queen Of The Gold Camps And Home Of The Famous Vigilantes"**
>
> **Bannack**

Beaverhead Rock is located about 7 miles south of Dillon and was named by Lewis and Clark during their expedition in 1805.

The Big Hole Battlefield National Historic Site, located just a few miles west of Wisdom, is the site of a major battle between the retreating Nez Perce, under Chief Joseph, and the U.S. Army. During a sad and tragic chapter in our American heritage, this Indian tribe made a heroic and masterful flight from Idaho to the Canadian border in 1877 while trying to evade capture by the military. For two months they attempted to elude the pursuing Army and volunteer forces led by Col. John Gibbon of the US 7th Infantry. At dawn on August 9, 1877, Gibbon attacked the 800 sleeping Nez Perce Indians camped on the Big Hole River at this site, and although many men, women and children of the tribe were killed, many managed to escape and continue towards Canada. The battlefield is open year-round and offers visitors an excellent self-guided trail tour and interesting interpretive center with audio-visual presentation and gift shop.

RECREATION

Beaverhead Golf and Country Club is a great nine hole course located at 1200 Hwy 41 and is managed by Pat Stish. Call 683-9933 for a tee time at this very well maintained public course with a clubhouse offering refreshments, sandwiches and a small, but complete, pro shop.

Elkhorn Hot Springs is located 43 miles north of Dillon in Polaris. This unique hot springs offers pure mountain water without the sulfuric smells so common elsewhere. The pool is open 10-10 and restaurant available 7 a.m. to 9 p.m. with a full menu of delightful meals. The mountains come right down to the edge of the pool and you just might see a moose walk by the fence. The main pool is bathtub-warm with a hotter version available alongside. Showers and hot tubs are inside the poolhouse for the day visitor with newly remodeled cabins and a rustic lodge available should you wish to stay. Of course, excellent fishing is close by and scenic hiking trails abound. Snowmobiling is enjoyed by many in the winter and you'll love the hunt for garnets and crystals in Crystal Park all year round just a few miles above the springs. A special treat and less than five minutes from the Maverick Ski Area, super downhill skiing only 45 minutes from Dillon.

Beaverhead Marina and RV Park is located at the Clark Canyon Reservoir just 20 miles south of Dillon on I-15. The man-made lake is eight square miles of outstanding year-round fishing with rainbow, brown trout and ling in abundance. Reportedly the home of the "big ones" where catches of 7 to 9 pound fish are not uncommon, it's also home of two major fish derbies on Father's Day and the Sunday after Super Bowl each year. Contact marina owners Richard and Carol Gossett at 683-5556 for details. A great neighbor to the full service marina, you'll enjoy excellent camping and great dining or a drink directly across the highway from the dam at the Buffalo Lodge.

SPECIAL EVENTS

Rancher Roundup Day, held each Memorial Day weekend, started as a fun event for the agricultural community surrounding Dillon and a chance for real cowboys and locals to show their stuff. The first event is now Rope-N-Stroke, a combination of golf and team roping. More traditional activities include large team roping and barrel racing. Teams of 6 people, including one girl, compete in great events like team branding, team penning, wild horse race, wild cow milking, saddle bronc riding. This is real ranch rodeo stuff and something you're likely to enjoy even more than professional rodeo.

> **"The First Event Is 'Rope-N-Stroke'"**
>
> **Rancher Roundup Days**

Bannack Days is held the 3rd weekend in July and includes two days of real pioneering activities. Events and displays include demonstrations of candle-making, soap making, and, of course, good food and good fun on this trip back in time. Locals are dressed in period costumes and you'll really enjoy the staged gun fights, hangings, gold panning and blackpowder contests. Good fun and lots to see.

> **"Gunfights, Hangings, Gold Panning, And Black Powder Contests"**
>
> **Bannack Days**

Dillon Jaycee Rodeo and Beaverhead County Fair held on Labor Day weekend is Dillon's main event. The fair opens on the Wednesday before Labor Day and is jam-packed with exhibits and events. Every day is a full schedule, and of course, since you're in ranching and cowboy country, horse and livestock events seem to take the lead. Billed as "Montana's Biggest Weekend," they work hard to make it a fact as the Jaycee Rodeo is held on Sunday and Monday and the streets are wall-to-wall people every night. Big name entertainment is held Monday night to finish off the event. A great event in a great Montana community! (Call the Chamber at 683-5511 for all event locations and times.)

EMERGENCY INFORMATION

Reliable service is available at College Exxon, 636 S. Atlantic, phone 683-5870; the Chevrolet dealer, Paul's Motors, 675 N. Montana, phone 683-2371; or the Ford dealer, Big Sky Motors, 790 N. Montana.

Barrett Memorial Hospital can help you with a problem at 1260 S. Atlantic. Call for an appointment at 683-2323 or use 911 for emergencies.

Your pet will be well taken care of at the Veterinary Hospital Inc., 935 S. Atlantic, phone 683-2385, where Dr. Knorr or Dr. Nelson can serve you.

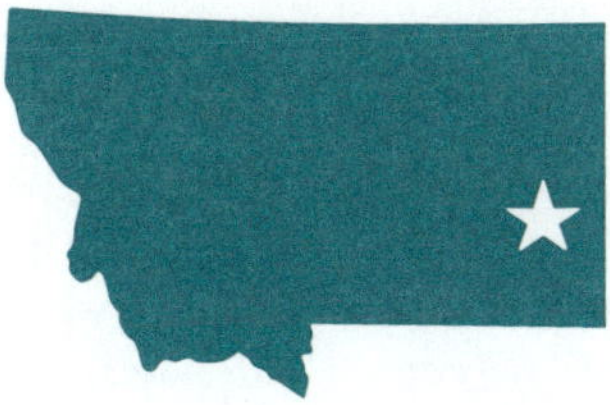

EKALAKA

The locals say, "Every night is like Saturday night and Saturday night is like the Fourth of July in Ekalaka." This southeastern Montana community was named for the daughter of the Sioux Chief Eagle Man. Her name was Ijakalaka and she was presented to David H. Russell in return for eight horses and a 100 pound sack of sugar. In the native tongue, Ijkalaka's name means "pick up and move." The area's economy is based on agriculture and ranching and many local operations raise registered cattle that attract buyers from all over the world to their bull sales. Tourist information is available from Morine Anderson who represents the chamber out of her home at 775-6658 or write Box 297, Ekalaka, Mt. 59324.

WHERE TO EAT

B & B Grill is operated by Bill and Bonnie Elmore, offers a relaxed atmosphere with nice surroundings, friendly waiters and super food. Specialties include steak and prime rib.

Wrangler N Cafe is open 5-12 and is operated by Mrs. Gay Ness where you'll enjoy trout, shrimp, halibut or regular favorites like steaks, chicken or burgers. Many locals order the exceptional red snapper or steak-shrimp combo.

"Exceptional Steak Shrimp Combo"

Wrangler N Cafe

Some great picnic areas are close at hand in Medicine Rocks Park, Ekalaka Park, and Camp Needmore, or in the Custer National Forest where it borders the town. Local Senior citizens often meet on Main Street for potluck meals and card games.

WHERE TO STAY

Guest House Motel is on Main Street and close to a store, the Old Stand Bar and the B & B Grill. The 12 unit facility is operated by Sam and Joyce Rutledge, former ranchers in the area who are a good source of information about local attractions and activities.

Camp Needmore is an indication of the special way this community takes care of its own. Located south of town just off Hwy 7, it was built by the CCC in the 30's and is used regularly for reunions, weddings and childrens camps. Cabins are rustic, containing only beds, however the kitchen is fully equipped with dishes, cooking utensils, walk-in cooler, freezer and the facility boasts tennis courts, dancing and dining areas. Good road to this very scenic area. Interested persons can contact Leslie Dean at 775-6513 for more information.

> "Great Spot For Reunions And Weddings"
>
> Camp Needmore

WHERE TO SHOP

Hughest Mainline Store is open 9-5:30 and is operated by Helen Hughest. Along with the usual things found in a department store, you'll enjoy the good selection of Black Hills gold and the warm, accommodating help from Helen.

Wear Hardware is owned and operated by Bill Wear from 8:30-5:30. Always helpful, you can count on Bill for the hardware and hunting supplies you're looking for and some friendly advice on how to enjoy the great out of doors around Ekalaka.

WATERING HOLES

Old Stand Bar is operated by Owen (Skeet) Hedges. A hang-out for locals and spot where ranchers gather to catch up on their problems, you won't find a friendlier place. A great watering hole since the late 1800's, the bar now offers coffee or iced tea as well. Of course, its a good place to try your luck at the poker machines or a game of pool.

The New Life Bar is operated by Kate Talkington and is located in a unique converted stone garage. A great stopping-off place, and if you see Kate, ask her about what kind of special fun she gets going on Saturday nights.

Buckhorn Bar is owned and operated by Marshall Kalstrom and is a quiet place to stop, have a drink and check out the local ranch brands on display. If you get a chance to visit with Bud, you'll greatly enjoy the wealth of local history he'll willingly share with you.

EXHIBITS

Carter County Museum is located on Main Street across from the local bank. It's open 1-4 Tues.-Sun., and curator is Marshall Lambert, a teacher and alumni from Princeton University and the University of Alaska. Literally filled with artifacts, including dinosaur remains from local digs, the place is a must-see. If you meet Marshall, you won't soon forget the experience.

> **"Complete Duck-Billed Dinosaur Skeleton On Display"**
>
> **Carter County Museum**

HISTORIC PLACES

Medicine Rocks Park is located north of Ekalaka on Highway 7 and offers a dramatic grouping of castle-like rock formations created by the erosion of sandstone. Over 300 acres in size, the park has a picnic area with tables, fresh water and restrooms. The name came from use of the area by Indians to "make medicine." Area was visited by Teddy Roosevelt and literally thousands of names and dates of other visitors are carved in the rocks. More information is available by calling Morine Anderson at 775-6658.

Ekalaka Park is about 7 miles south of town in the Custer National Forest. Located in a deep, wooded draw with tables, fresh water and restrooms, it's a cool, secluded spot you will enjoy on a hot summer day. Morine Anderson can help you with more information by calling 775-6658.

SPECIAL EVENTS

The Meadowlark Club holds its semiannual celebration to honor the Montana state bird's return and departure in the spring and fall. Parades, prizes, games, barbecue, potluck dinner and dances are just part of the fun that begins at the Old Stand Bar. Contact Skeet Hedges at 775-6661 or Janice Markuson at 775-6348 for this year's dates and times.

Carter County "Days of '85" is scheduled for the second weekend in August each year and is held at the same time as the fair and 4-H events. A parade culminates the affair on Sunday, and the event honors the community's beginning in 1885.

Carter County Wagon Train can offer an exciting and unique look at what it was like before gasoline engines, radios and tight schedules. Call Keith Larson at 775-6273 or write Box 275, Ekalaka, MT. 59324 for details.

EMERGENCY INFORMATION

Fruit Repair and Service offers reliable car care from 8-6 daily. Owners are Troy and Mikel Fruit, phone 775-6542. Dahl Memorial Hospital and Clinic is located downtown, south of the Courthouse. Open 24 hours; call 775-8730 for help.

Medicine Rock Veterinary Clinic is located a mile north of town on Hwy 7. Greg Tooke is DVM and can be reached at 775-6494 or 775-6493. He flies his own plane to his customers and has lots of experience with both small and large animals.

FLORENCE

Florence, the first community you reach as you enter the beautiful Bitterroot Valley, is located 20 miles south of Missoula on Hwy 93. The valley offers a uniquely mild Montana climate and is the second fastest-growing area in the state. Celebrities like Hank Williams Jr. are finding it a great place to live and locals tout a quality of life second-to-none. Spectacular scenery abounds and tourist information is available from 9-5 at the Chamber of Commerce, 105 E. Main or by calling 363-2400.

WHERE TO EAT

Six Pac at 5303 S. Hwy 93 is an excellent supper club with a good menu. Jayne Willet starts serving at 5 and locals like the great salad bar, prime rib and Sunday brunch. Call 273-9921 for reservations.

Dee Dee's Drive-In at 5502 Old Hwy 93 is operated by Royal and Vicki Crawford and offers great food in a non-smoking environment. Specialties include burgers and pizza. If you see Royal, ask for a tour of the taxidermy shop next door.

SHOPPING

Tie Chute Art Gallery on Hwy 93 is operated by Colleen and Joseph Tribble and open 10-5. A great gallery offering a wide variety of western art, prints and excellent framing. Call 273-2695 for more information.

BARS AND CASINOS

Bum Steer on Hwy 93 is operated by Shirley Richardson and opens at 11 daily.

Rustic Hut on Hwy 93 opens at 12 and is run by Fred Peters. It is a hang out for younger people and has pool tables and poker machines.

Six Pac has a bar and casino separate from dining area. Opens at 5. See Where to Eat.

EXHIBITS

Lee Metcalf Wildlife Refuge, near Stevensville, is definitely something worth checking into.

HISTORIC PLACES

Marcus Daly Mansion is located in Hamilton. Copper King Marcus Daly built the mansion and stables on the outskirts of Hamilton and tours are given daily. Contact the Chamber for details.

"Copper King's Magnificent Home"

Marcus Daly Mansion

St. Mary's Mission in Stevensville is interesting and available for viewing.

RECREATION

Stevensville Golf Course is a 9 hole course north of town and surrounded by the Lee Metcalf Wildlife Refuge. Great golfing and a unique experience.

Hamilton Golf Course offers 18 holes of great golf and is located SE of town on Hwy 93. Call 363-4251 for tee times or more information.

EMERGENCY INFORMATION

Marcus Daly Hospital in Hamilton serves the area at 1200 Westwood Drive, 363-2211. In case of emergency dial 911.

Victor Veterinary Clinic is open 8-5 in Victor MT, phone 642-3471.

FORSYTH

Frequently known as the "City of Trees," Forsyth is the county seat of Rosebud County and locals say Custer was the real loser when he turned 10 miles east to meet his demise and missed Forsyth's beautiful valley. The city of about 2500 is situated on I-94, 100 miles east of Billings, 46 miles west of Miles City and 100 miles southeast of Roundup. Coal development has helped the community maintain a steady growth and although the economic base is still agriculture, it's now compliment-ed by an Air Force SAC training center. Tourist Information is available at 188 N. 9th where Mike Blakesley at Valley Auto Supply can answer your questions. He's available 9-5 Mon.-Fri. at 356-2141.

WHERE TO EAT

The Blue Spruce Cafe at 109 S. 10th is a family restaurant with friendly atmosphere and good food. Manager Phil Evans' breakfast caramel rolls or homemade soups won't disappoint you. Soft ice cream and yogurt cones are a great treat in the summer.

The Famous Jersey Lilly is located in Ingomar, 41 miles NW of Forsyth on Hwy 12. This nationally publicized restaurant has a great rustic western atmosphere and offers good food and great company. Be sure to try the Sheepherder hors d' oeuvres or Bill's bean soup. If you see him, be sure to ask about his days as a chef or a few memorable moments in the boxing ring.

"Outstanding Sheepherder Hors d' oeuvres"

The Jersey Lilly—Ingomar

The Lions Club meets at the Blue Spruce every Monday at noon except during June, July and August. Guest Lions are welcome.

A nice place to picnic is Riverside Park located north of the public high school. Facilities include picnic tables, indoor heated pool and restrooms. Nearby camping areas are maintained by Fish, Wildlife and Parks and are located on the banks of the Yellowstone River on the northwest edge of town, or in the north central part of Forsyth itself.

WHERE TO STAY

Best Western Sundowner Inn at 1018 Front Street has 28 units and is centrally located in the business district just across the street from a family restaurant and near convenience stores. Call Joe Wilson for reservations at 356-2115.

Westwind Motor Inn at 225 Westwind Lane is a modern motel with 33 units just off I-94 and Hwy 12. Gary Oakland and Howard Ullman own the operation, phone 356-2038.

Rail's Inn Motel at 3rd and Front Street is owned by Bunkes, Inc., has 50 units and offers restaurant and bar. Call 356-2242.

SHOPPING

V-Store Trading Post at 863 Main Street, owned and operated by Robert and Diane Kalt, is open daily except Sunday. You'll enjoy this stop where you'll find anything and everything you used to see in that old dime store.

Yellowstone Pharmacy at 1025 Main is open Mon.-Sat. and owned by Neil and Sharon Donner. One of the very first commercial downtown buildings is now converted into a drug store that reportedly can match anything New York has to offer.

Shy Ann's at 927 Main St. is a nice gift and novelty shop run by Pat Eve, open daily except Sunday.

WATERING HOLES

Buff's Bar at 845 Main St. is owned and operated by Jack Snyder. Bar and Casino has silver dollars imbedded in the bar counter and an interesting display of tropical fish. Food is available and the homemade soup is a great treat. If Jack's around, ask him about his sheep herding days.

> **"Ask Jack About His Sheepherding Days"**
>
> **Bufff's Bar**

Lariat Bar at 971 Main is owned by Greg Reid and features big-screen television for great sporting events viewing.

Lady Luck Lounge and Casino offers great gaming and all that Town Pump provides at 974 Front Street.

EXHIBITS

Rosebud County Pioneer Museum on Main Street, directly east of the County Courthouse, is open spring, summer and fall. Attractively presented collection of local artifacts.

HISTORIC PLACES

Rosebud County Courthouse on Main Street between 12th and 13th is a replica of the Montana State Capitol in Helena and is on the National Register of Historic Landmarks.

The town of Ingomar, MT is located 41 miles NW on Hwy 12. Once known as the sheep capital of the world, Ingomar is now home to the famous Jersey Lilly Cafe, featured in many major magazines and newspapers. The facility is owned by William "Bill" Seward and still sports boardwalks and outhouses. A must stop you will enjoy.

RECREATION

Forsyth Municipal Golf Course is located two miles SW of town on the Frontage Road. The beautiful 9 hole golf course is well maintained, with grass greens, and has a club house with

"Beautiful Nine-Hole Course"

Forsyth Municipal Golf Course

bar and restaurant. Lunches are available during the golf season and tee times are a good idea; phone 356-7710. Interesting layout you will enjoy.

Hunting and fishing are big business in Forsyth, and you'll find outstanding antelope, deer and upland bird hunting. Literally one of those places where you can walk just a few steps from your vehicle and find yourself smack in the middle of ducks, geese, pheasants, grouse, partridge and turkeys. The Yellowstone River flows along the north edge of town and offers good river fishing.

SPECIAL EVENTS

The Rosebud-Treasure County Fair is held each August and is a good time for all. Contact the Fair Association Office at 356-2144 for dates and details.

Forsyth Duck Days, an annual fundraiser for the Chamber of Commerce, is held in the city park just west of town in July. Event includes wagering on the destiny of rubber ducks released into the Yellowstone and a street dance Saturday night.

EMERGENCY INFORMATION

Heberle Ford can take good care of car problems at 1825 Front Street, 356-2221. This full service shop also has a wrecker.

Rosebud Community Hospital has 24 hour care at 383 N. 17th Ave. Call 356-2161 for appointment or 911 in an emergency. Air ambulance service is also available if necessary.

Yellowstone Valley Veterinary Clinic is located at 1227 Front St. and is open Mon.-Sat., phone 356-7564. Dr. Gerald Killen will take good care of your pet.

FRENCHTOWN

Frenchtown is located about 15 miles west of Missoula on I-90 and because it was settled by farmers and ranchers of French descent, the name Frenchtown held. Many descendants of the original settlers still live in the valley with road names such as Touchette, LaCasse and Marcure still common. Most residents work in Missoula, yet seem to treasure the rural lifestyle of the Frenchtown Valley. The school system is touted as one of the best in the state and many family-owned farms are passed down from generation to generation. Hay, grain, cattle and sheep are still the main source of income, but Stone Container, a large liner-board wood-pulp mill, is the largest employer and located just south of town.

WHERE TO EAT

Nine Mile House on Nine Mile Road at Exit 82 off I-90 is run by Doug and Barb Gaut and offers great western atmosphere, excellent food, with prime rib the specialty of the house. Open everyday with all you can eat ribs on Monday nights, you'll enjoy this Montana roadhouse with a full service bar. Call 626-5668 for reservations.

> **"Wonderful Western Atmosphere And Very Special Prime Rib"**
>
> **Nine-Mile House**

Coffee Cup Cafe in the Frenchtown Shopping Center is ownedby Glenn and Sue Green and Managed by Diane Zuraff. Open from 7 a.m. til 8 p.m. Mon-Sat and 8-2 on Sundays, it's the place where many locals meet and eat in Frenchtown, and you can't miss with the daily special. Homemade pies/desserts are always great. If you're hungry, try the Bronc Burger.

SHOPPING

Mountain Homestead at the I-90 W. Ninemile Exit is open seasonally and operated by Rene Cyr and Jolene Sherry. The old mountain homestead of the Cyr family, this uniquely restored facility is operated as a gift and craft shop with many items made by the family. Excellent assortment of country crafts.

WATERING HOLES

Frenchtown Club just off I-90 West exit is run by Rocky Zavarelli and offers great small town atmosphere. You'll find Rocky's kitchen serves excellent meals at reasonable prices. Specialties include Chester Fried Chicken and a prime rib sandwich that's a real meal. Enjoy cold beer on tap, well drinks and live music most weekends. A big community supporter, Rocky usually has a fundraiser going and if you meet him, ask about airplanes and luck.

> **"Ask Rocky About Airplanes And Luck"**
>
> **Frenchtown Club**

Alcan Bar and Cafe is on Beckwith and run by Steve, Betty and Mike Bidlake. A friendly tavern with a pool table and lots of gaming machines, live music on special occasions and street dances in the summer. The Alcan also has good daily lunch and dinner specials at great prices.

Larry's Six Mile Tavern at the Huson-Six Mile Exit off I-90 is known for its great chicken, burgers and country style BBQ Ribs on Thursday night for only $4.50. They run out early, so be there at 6. The tavern is owned and operated by Larry and Phyllis Bardwell.

HISTORIC PLACES

Nine Mile Ranger Station is located at Ninemile Exit off I-90, 5 miles west of Frenchtown. Follow the signs up Ninemile Road to one of the oldest active ranger stations in Montana. Daily tours are available, as are walking trails, picnic areas and a gift shop. This is the home of the "Fire Fighting Mules."

RECREATION

Frenchtown Pond is located off the I-90 Exit, then left along the Frontage Road for about 1/2 mile. Although no overnight parking is allowed, this great local summer recreation area has picnicking, swimming and fishing. A nice place to cool off and stretch your legs.

King Ranch Golf Course now offers nine scenic holes of golf, driving range, practice green, pro shop along with excellent restaurant and lounge. Greg VanNatta can make you a tee time or give you a lesson and owners Todd and Trudy Green can point out a wonderful variety of critters that call the course home. The view from the clubhouse is like watching a wildlife video and makes for great entertainment while dining.

Clark's Fork River runs through the whole valley. A couple nice places to stop and wet a line are Erskine and Petty Creek Fishing Accesses. To get to Erskine, take the Frenchtown exit into town, then west to Mullan Road, then right and follow the signs. The Petty Creek Access is right at the Petty Creek exit off I-90, the first exit in Alberton. A boat ramp is available and there's great fishing on either the Clark's Fork or Petty Creek.

> **"Great Spot To Stop And Wet A Line"**
>
> **Erskine Fishing Access**

White Water Rafting trips are available through Western Waters River Trips. Owner Jerry Nichols has 16 years experience in the business, and will guarantee you a safe excursion with lots of fun. Day or overnight trips are available with meals provided and fishing during season. A great bonus is the wildlife viewing and gorgeous scenery. Select the Alberton Gorge trip if you're after excitement. Operation is open May 15 through mid October.

SPECIAL EVENTS

Enjoy the School House Christmas and Easter Open Houses each weekend during the Christmas and Easter seasons at the Schoolhouse Bed and Breakfast located about two miles up Ninemile Road. You'll find great European style gifts, handmade wooden toys and hand-painted items by local artists. Unusual crafts abound and the Christmas show is especially well known for its nativity scenes from all around the world. People come from all over Montana to browse and enjoy lunch (available only limited days during Christmas Season). Owners Lester and Hanneke Ippish travel the world over for ideas and are very interesting to talk to. Call Lester or Hanneke at 626-5879 for more details or a reservation for a wonderful night in their Bed and Breakfast open weekends most of the year.

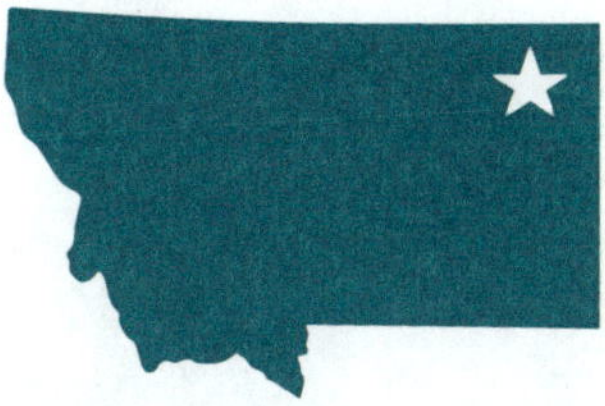

FROID

Froid means "cold" in French and is a farm-ranch community of 200 hardy souls located 20 miles west of the North Dakota line and 50 miles south of the Canadian border. The town was founded in 1910 as a trading spot for homesteaders, and some of the world's best cattle and spring wheat are raised in the area. Much of local recreation centers around the schools with athletics and speech-debate great sources of pride for students who are bused from as far away as 20 miles. Tourist information is available from Greg Wallander, secretary/treasurer of the Froid Commercial Club, Box 128, Froid, MT or call 766-2357, 8 to 5 weekdays.

WHERE TO EAT

Mint Bar and Cafe on Main Street is open 7-7 Mon.-Thurs., 7-9 Fri.-Sat. and 7 to 2 Sun. Owner is Jan Peters and the place is well known for its great sirloin steak, prime rib and outstanding cookies, pies and rolls.

Annex Bar on Main Street serves pizza and chicken and is owned by Ed Reiter.

> **"Well Known For Its Sirloin Steak And Prime Rib"**
>
> Mint Bar and Cafe

WHERE TO STAY

No commercial accommodations for travelers are found in Froid but private homes are available for hunters and can be arranged through Jan Peters at 766-9955.

WHERE TO SHOP

Hunting and fishing equipment can be found at the Coast to Coast on Main Street, phone 766-2313. The old-fashioned hardware store carries most items to fix anything and is open 8:30-5:30 except Sundays. Owner Dave Quammen or manager Joyce Bakken can be counted on for friendly help and reliable advice. If you see Dave, don't get him started on politics unless you're prepared for a heated discussion.

Edie's on Main Street is open 9 to 5:30 except Sundays and has good selection of books, magazines and sundries. If you see owner Edie, ask her if she misses England.

WATERING HOLES

Mint Bar on Main Street is open 9-1 except alternating Sundays and owner Jan Peters can give you good idea of what's happening around Froid.

Annex Bar downtown is owned by Ed Reiter, open 9-1 except alternate Sundays and offers pizza and chicken with beer, wine, hard drinks and dancing on occasion. If things are a little slow and you see Ed, get him talking about sports. He's a real fan and loves a heated discussion.

EXHIBITS

Medicine Lake Wildlife Refuge is located 8 miles north of town and two miles south of Medicine Lake. Outstanding place to view nesting and migratory birds including an occasional trumpeter swan. Great nature trails and viewing tower. Call 789-2305 for seasonal information.

"Picturesque Nature Trails And Convenient Viewing Tower"

Medicine Lake Wildlife Refuge

RECREATION

Outstanding hunting for pheasants, grouse and deer in the area. Contact Greg Sunwall at 766-2357 8-5 weekdays for local information. Many farmers and ranchers are cooperating with Montana Fish and Wildlife programs to provide access to private lands on a controlled basis.

SPECIAL EVENTS

Jeff Ryder Memorial Basketball Tournament is held annually in the Froid Gym during the month of March. The three day tourney attracts some outstanding college and semi-pro players with most of proceeds going to a local scholarship fund. A truly outstanding all-you-can-eat fish feed is held by the Rod and Gun Club in conjunction with the tournament. Call Jan Peters or Ed Reiter at 766-2221 for details.

> **"Watch Outstanding College And Semi-Pro Players"**
>
> **Jeff Ryder Memorial Tournament**

Gust Fjeseth Memorial Softball Tournament is held in June each year. Three day slow pitch tournament attracts players from a wide area. Call Jan Peters at 766-2221 to find out how to participate.....or watch.

Lutheran Church Lutefisk Supper is held at the Lutheran Church on Main Street. Exceptional Scandinavian feast offering lutefisk (a fish that has been preserved in lye, rinsed and boiled, with an excellent taste if you can get past the smell) or meatballs for the faint of heart. Lots of homemade Norwegian pastries for all.

EMERGENCY INFORMATION

Lodahl Farm and Auto Repair on Main Street can take care of your car or RV needs. Pete Lodahl is owner and hours are 8-5 Mon.-Sat., phone 766-2420.

Nearest medical facilities are at Roosevelt Memorial Hospital in Culbertson, 14 miles south of Froid.

ENNIS

A town of about 800, Ennis is located on the Madison River and is surrounded by snow capped mountains. Established in the late 1800's and for years primarily an agricultural supply hub, the largest employer these days is the Two Tale Mine in the Cameron area. Several of the current businesses were started by pioneer families and many still retain the country store atmosphere and old fashioned courtesy. The town has real appeal as an authentic western community offering first class attractions and accommodations. Ennis, Virginia City and Nevada City are all an easy hour's drive from the west entrance of Yellowstone, America's first national park. Visitors come from miles around to enjoy the exceptional hiking trails, hunting, golfing, water skiing, cross country skiing and snowmobiling. Tourist information is available from the Ennis Chamber of Commerce, Box 291, Ennis, MT, 59720, or by contacting Ed Williams at the town hall at 682-4287.

"Exceptional Hiking Trails, Hunting, Golfing, Water Skiing, Cross Country Skiing And Snowmobiling"

WHERE TO EAT

Continental Divide Restaurant on Main Street is excellent and owners Jay and Karen Bentley offer fresh seafood regularly. If you see Jay, ask about his Cajun special.

Kathy's of Course on Main Street has outstanding homemade soup and fresh-baked bread. Some selections sure to please include the soup special, Philly

Steak Sandwich, Vegetarian Sandwich and Black Bottom Cupcakes.

> **"Mouth Watering Philly Steak Sandwich"**
>
> **Kathy's of Course**

Ennis Cafe is great local gathering spot located on Main Street. Owners Jack and Darlene Kristovich offer daily lunch special, great Sunday dinner special and outstanding fresh strawberry pie.

Ennis Lions Club Park is great picnic spot located at the south entrance to town. If you have kids with you, they'll enjoy the playground or even a chance at a trout - there are more than a few big ones left in the park's kids' fishing pond.

WHERE TO STAY

El Western Motel is located about 1/2 mile south of Ennis on Highway 287 south, run by Ted and Bobby Bjork, phone 682-4217, and offers spectacular view in a quiet setting with small, nostalgic log cabins. Very clean with manicured lawn and even a putting green. You'll find rates at this 20 unit motel a great value and if you see Bobby ask her about their last People to People trip.

Hickey's Motel managed by Mike and Mandy Cerino is right downtown on Main Street, phone 682-4378. It has 20 units, is reasonably priced and features outdoor pool, hot tub and kitchen units.

Silvertip Lodge owned and operated by Dick and Kate Barr is located downtown on Main Street, phone 682-4384, has 12 units and offers clean economical accommodations.

Rainbow Valley Motel at south entrance to Ennis, phone 682-4264, will let you enjoy the peace and quiet of being out of town, while still near the business district. The motel is owned and operated by Ed and Jeanne Williams and offers 20 units, some with kitchenettes. The outdoor pool is wonderful on a hot summer afternoon and

> **"Spectacular View, Quiet Setting And Great Rates"**
>
> **El Western Motel**

you'll appreciate the great mountain view and exceptional cleanliness. The Rainbow Valley stays open year round and will board horses during hunting season.

Sportsman's Lodge is on Hwy #287 as you enter Ennis from the North, managed by Stephanie Vujovich and offers a special rustic cabin for those who want something different or real comfort in the 30 newly remodeled units. An outdoor pool is available and if you want to relax before dinner in the lodge's dining room, you will enjoy the western hospitality of the basement bar. Good food and great service.

Riverside Motel on Main Street is just a two minute walk from Lions Club Park and the Madison River. Owned and operated by Bob and Elsie Hines, the 14 unit motel is clean, convenient and economical.

9T9 Ranch Bed and Breakfast at 90 Gravelly Range Road, phone 682-7659, is located midway up the Madison Valley, where you can view a full fifty miles of the majestic Madison Range. Wildlife abounds just outside the three guest rooms that share a sitting room and you'll revel at the outstanding food. Owners Vaughn and Judy Herrick will make your stay truly memorable as you savor Judy's fresh baked pastries, special granola and in-season fruit bowl or Vaughn's sumptuous omelets with hashbrowns or biscuits and gravy with eggs. Box lunches are available. You'll enjoy a walk to the river for premier rainbow or brown fly-fishing, and float trips arranged by the Herricks are outstanding. Families are welcome and you'll not soon forget the Montana hospitality that will make your stay at the 9T9 a special experience.

"Enjoy Vaughn's Sumptuous Omelets"

9T9 Ranch Bed and Breakfast

WHERE TO SHOP

Benjie's on Main Street is owned and operated by Benjie and Jim Engebretsen, phone 682-4689. Great gifts, books, bags and good buys on sterling silver jewelry.

Ennis Rock House on Hwy 287 is owned by Neil and Ida Brandon, phone 682-4689. Unique gold mountings, gemstones, and silver smithing.

Ennis Trading Post on Main Street, 682-4329, is managed by Phyllis Bowles and offers western clothing for men and women, with an interesting collection of Indian jewelry and gift items.

Hole-In-The-Wall Art Gallery on Main Street, 682-7235, has a large selection of original artwork, bronze sculptures, prints, Indian jewelry, pottery and antler art. Owned and operated by Lee and Lathie Poole, managed by Kathy Sposita.

Madison River Fishing Company on Main Street is owned and operated by Tom and Nancy Dimeola. A full-service fly shop with guides and fly fishing school available. Call 1-800-227-7127 for a free 40-page catalog.

Nearly New Shop on Main Street is operated by the Madison Valley Women's Club. Offers used clothing and interesting collectibles at low prices.

The Depot on Main Street is owned and managed by Vicki Lubke and offers heartwarming gifts, unusual toys, children's clothing and kitchenware. A great gift shop.

WATERING HOLES

Claim Jumper Saloon on Main is owned and operated by Kelly and Brad DiIorio, phone 682-7454. Enjoy shuffle board, pool, poker machines, live bands and great food in the back at TC's Restaurant.

Longbranch Saloon on Main is owned by Sam and Chris Johnson. The western bar has pool tables, gaming machines and live cards. Good supper club in the back.

Silver Dollar Saloon on Main is run by Bob and Sherry McDonald. Great Bar-B-Q Ribs in the back with pool tables; gaming machines up front.

EXHIBITS

The Ennis National Fish Hatchery is located 12 miles from Ennis. Call manager Wes Orr at 682-4847 for directions and hours. The life of a fish from fingerling to trophy catch can be viewed as fish raised here are transplanted in rivers and lakes throughout the West. If you see Wes ask him about his Boy Scout snipe hunts!

Wildlife Museum of the West on Main in Ennis is a must see and is owned by Larry and Stephanie Altimus. Animals of the western U.S. are nicely displayed in their natural surroundings. Larry is a taxidermist, has his own taxidermy shop and is a great source for local information at 682-7141.

HISTORIC PLACES

Virginia City and Nevada City are just 14 miles SW of Ennis and offer a unique experience Memorial Day through Labor Day each year. Revisit the historic West as you saunter down boardwalks peeking in windows of the many nostalgic stores. Catch the train to Nevada City to pan for gold, take in the Virginia City Players at the old theater or see the Brewery Show, a hilarious evening of vaudeville acts. Many other attractions just too numerous to list. A must see if you're in the area.

Old Indian Trail on the east shore of Ennis Lake is a unique opportunity to hike the authentic Indian trail connecting the mountain ranges of the Madison and the Gallatin drainages.

RECREATION

Beartrap Express in Ennis offers mild to exciting white water rafting through the scenic Bear Trap Canyon. Call Johnny France at 682-7216 for more information. Great fun!

Madison Meadows Golf Club, Call Harry Liss or Mary Mattson at 682-7468 for directions to this picturesque nine hole golf course. Completed in 1982, it's one of Montana's most interesting and was designed by Frank Hummel. Carts and club rentals available. An annual Skins Golf Tournament is a great event the last weekend in June.

"Picturesque Frank Hummel Course"

Madison Meadows Golf Club

SPECIAL EVENTS

Annual Hunters Feed on Main Street is held in October the Friday before the big game hunting season opens. Marc Glines at 682-4357 has more information and samples from the Wild Game Cooking Contest are reason enough for dropping in.

Pioneer Days offers old-fashioned family fun with a weekend of games. Young and old enjoy dress your dog contests, pie eating events, chain saw contests, bubble gum blowing contests and Buffalo BAR-B-Q in the park. Call the Chamber at 682-4287 for dates and times.

The July 3rd and 4th Rodeo and Parade is a fun-filled, action-packed celebration. Evening rodeo on the 3rd, parade on the 4th at 9:30 with rodeo at 2. The very special Madison County Sidesaddle Club is a great local attraction.

EMERGENCY INFORMATION

D & D Auto Shop in town at 682-4234 offers reliable help 8-5 Mon.-Sat. Owners Dan and Dennis Dedman operate full-service auto and tire repair shop.

Madison Valley Clinic and Hospital on Hwy 287 offers 24 hour care with clinic at 682-4223 and Hospital and emergency at 682-4222. Three doctors, a fully equipped emergency room and a 12 bed hospital serve the community.

White and White Veterinarian Hospital is located at 5098 U.S. Highway 287, phone is 682-7151 and regular hours are from 8-5 Mon.-Fri. and 8-12 Sat. Call same number for emergency. Full service, state-of-the-art small animal hospital with boarding available.

HARLOWTON

Located in the heart of antelope country, Harlowton remembers its railroad roots with the E-57B Electric Engine Park and restoration is progressing on the former Milwaukee Depot. The town is kept strong by its farm and ranch economy, and the locals seem more than willing to help each other, promote a project or just enjoy a visit over a cup of coffee. The town comes to life for its annual Fourth of July celebration with rodeos, parades and fireworks. Tourist information is available at the Harlowton Public Library or by contacting Kathy Frost at 632-5523 9-12 and 1-5 Mon.-Fri.

WHERE TO EAT

The Cornerstone at 11 N. Central Ave is open 11-7 Mon.-Tue., 11-8 Wed.-Sat. and is operated by Tim (Sonny) Stinson and Joan. Locals love the pizza or Mexican specials on Saturday and a great treat is the fettucine with shrimp, crab and cheese. If you meet Sonny, ask him if Elway can get the job done next year.

The Crazy Mountain Inn in Martinsdale is located about 25 miles west of Harlowton and open daily except Monday and Tuesday. Owners Peter and Cheryl Marchi prepare great meals and everything's homemade, from dinner rolls to the cheesecake. Specialties include chicken fried steak and a truly great cheeseburger with fries. Call 632-4600 for more on this wonderful, out-of-the-way place.

"Everything's Homemade... From Dinner Rolls To Cheesecake"

Crazy Mountain Inn—Martinsdale

WHERE TO STAY

Graves Hotel has 48 rooms at 106 S. Central Ave., is owned by Dan Buckley and is listed on the National Historic Register. Built in 1908, the hotel offers a step back in time for visitors, but you won't be disappointed, many rooms have been renovated. Phone is 632-5855.

> **"Listed On The National Historic Register"**
>
> The Graves Hotel

Country Side Inn at 309 3rd NE, 632-4119, is an 11 unit motel owned and operated by Larry and Linda Schock. Facility has non-smoking rooms, cable TV, complimentary coffee and some refrigerators.

Troy Motel has 7 units at 106 2nd NE, 632-4428. Ron and Patty Vernholm operate this clean, accommodating stopping off place. Units have refrigerators and microwaves.

SHOPPING

Ray's Sports, Western Wear and Convenience Store on Highway 12 E. is open 9-6 Mon.-Sat., 10-5 on Sunday and offers a great selection of western clothing, jewelry, boots and an abundance of items for the sports enthusiast. You won't believe the inventory and if you see owner Alma Hinand, ask her for the low down on the great "Harlo" rodeo.

Point 'n Place at 112 N. Central is open 1-5 Mon-Sat and operated by Nancy Stoltz. Great selection of gift items, many painted and hand crafted by Nancy, who also teaches painting in evening classes.

The Toggery at 25 S. Central is open 9-5:30 Mon-Sat and operated by Phyllis and Duane Kolman. You'll enjoy good selection of women's clothing and display cases filled with unusual jewelry. Phyllis is great with her window displays and if you get to meet her, be sure to ask about Du and Poo.

Western Antiques at 107 2nd NE is owned and operated by Harvey and Evelyn Barney and open May to October from 10-5:30 daily except Sun and Wed. Place is packed full of nice, clean antiques and you'll enjoy the owners' gift of gab!

WATERING HOLES

Stockman's Bar at 17 N. Central Avenue is operated by Harry and Sharyn Klock and 'the' place to be in Harlo on Friday night. Great backbar, popular poker and keno machines and a CD jukebox.

Graves Hotel and Lounge at 106 S. Central is open at 11 daily and managed by Clara Jo Jacobson. Nice place to stop, have a drink, wander into the dining room for a meal or check in overnight.

The Argonaut is located east of Harlowton, run by William and Loretta Leuthold and open noon-2 in the summer and 3 p.m. to 2 a.m. in the winter. Great atmosphere inside this circular log building with attached game room featuring foosball and an electronic car kids love. Of course, poker and keno machines, too.

EXHIBITS

Upper Musselshell Historical Society Museum at 11 S. Central Ave. is open 10-5 Tue.-Sat. and 1-5 on Sun., May-Nov. Operated by Dolores Gillen, phone 632-5519, you'll enjoy three levels of exhibits that include an old school room, general store and kitchen, living room and bedroom of an early day home. Excellent collection of arrowheads and Indian relics. Don't miss the locally excavated dinosaur fossils and if you see Delores, ask her to point out the two headed calf and human skeleton if you missed them.

"Excellent Collection Of Indian Relics"

Upper Musselshell Historical Society Museum

Centennial Pioneer Family Bronze Sculpture is on permanent display on the Courthouse Lawn. The life-sized official Montana Centennial Sculpture is entitled "And They Called The Land Montana." Displayed is a wagon wheel that played a significant role in Montana's development; a young lad, our future, curious about life; a hard working mother dedicated to her family ; and an honest man kneeling upon the land they call home. Family strength and love were important to these folks who lived in isolation and Montana artist Mike Capser has done an outstanding job of depicting this great theme.

HISTORIC PLACES

Milwaukee Depot at the Bottom of Main Street is being restored by the City-County Preservation Committee and contact person is Warren Elwood at 632-5666. The Depot at one time served as the outpost for Harlowton's railroad livelihood and a railroad "goat" has been moved to the site.

E-57B Engine Park is on US 12 at Central Ave and commemorates the Milwaukee Railroad that served this area for over 75 years. Erected and maintained as a community project, it's typical of the public spirit possessed by the resourceful and independent local residents.

RECREATION

Jawbone Creek Country Club at the top of Main Street is a 9 hole grass green golf course with carts available for $6 and greens fees of $8 for 9 holes or $12 for all day. Visa is accepted and pop, beer, snacks and hamburgers are available at the club house. Call Dorene Tierney or Jim Bell at 632-9960 for a tee time at this great course.

Harlowton is located in the heart of antelope country and opens the season with a man-sized chicken fried steak feed the Saturday night before opening day. The affair is called the Hunters Feed and it's held at the Moose Lodge, 33 A. Ave. NE where you can feast from 6 till it's all gone.

The country around Harlowton is a hunting paradise with deer, ducks, geese, pheasants and most other rangeland birds. Trout fishing is plentiful at area lakes and streams. Nearby Deadman's Basin Reservoir is a man made lake offering boating, fishing and excellent windsurfing.

"Super Boating, Fishing And Windsurfing"

Deadman's Basin Reservoir

SPECIAL EVENTS

July 3rd and 4th Celebration is held annually in Chief Joseph Park and includes an afternoon parade and evening rodeo on the 3rd and morning parade, afternoon rodeo and evening fireworks display on the 4th. Contact Howard Holloway at 632-4277 for more information.

The July 4th Wagon Train event is organized by Janie Carlson and Ron Parrish, phone 632-5719 or 632-4150. Wagons gather on a local ranch south of town a few days before the 4th of July. The first night's camp at Lebo Lake features a pitchfork Fondue supper open to the public. The second night features a street dance in Two Dot with the last leg to Harlowton timed to join the parade on the 3rd.

Crazy Days and Craft Fair is held on Main Street every year on the first Saturday after Labor Day. Central Avenue is blocked off to traffic and craft booths are set up with businesses bringing out their Crazy Days specials and booths with baked goods, face painting and produce to create a festive occasion. Contact Julie Wojtowick at 632-5591 for details.

“Lebo Lake Pitchfork Fondue”

July 4 Wagon Train

EMERGENCY INFORMATION

Wojtowick Auto Repair at 119 2nd NE is full service station that won’t disappoint you. Open 9-5 Mon-Fri, owner Tim Wojtowick can be reached at 632-5591. Towing is available at Gordon’s Auto Repair, phone 632-4560.

Wheatland Memorial Hospital and Bair Memorial Clinic, both at 530 3rd NW, phone 632-4351 or 632-4343. Clinic is open 10-12 and 2-5 Mon.-Fri. and emergency care is available 24 hours a day by calling 911.

Holloway’s Veterinary Hospital is located south of town and is open 8-5 Mon.-Sat. Call 632-4371 for appointment or 632-4277 for emergency help.

LAUREL

Located in the beautiful Yellowstone Valley, Laurel's 6500 residents seem to like the advantages of small town living only 15 minutes from Montana's largest city. Although more than half of Laurel's citizens commute to jobs in Billings, serving the farmers who grow sugar beets and corn in the broad, sheltered valley irrigated by water from the Yellowstone still provides the backbone for the local economy. Other major employers include Montana Rail Link's large switching yard and the Cenex Refinery. Good schools, neighbors that still take the time to say hello and a location only minutes away from much of the recreation that makes living in Montana special sets Laurel apart in the Big Sky Country. Tourist information is available at the Chamber of Commerce office at 415 E. Main St. in the Laurel Outlook Newspaper Building. Hours are limited, so call first, phone is 628-8105.

WHERE TO EAT

Owl Diner is found downtown at 203 E. Main and offers small town diner atmosphere with good food, good prices and good service. Daily specials include soup or salad, main course, drink and dessert for under $4.00. Can't miss with the burgers; locals love their hot pork sandwiches. No friendlier waitresses anywhere.

Locomotive Restaurant and Casino is located at 216 First Ave. S., 628-7969. Serving breakfast, lunch and dinner, you'll find nice atmosphere and good food. Drinks are available and poker machines are far enough away not to distract from the quiet comfortable surroundings.

El Rancho is located about 5 miles south of Laurel on 310 in Silesia, phone 962-3251. Henry and Sally Rodriguez have operated this family owned roadhouse for over 20 years and offer a great Mexican and American menu. If you aren't in the mood for the terrific Mexican selections, try the huge portion of scallops. Sally still does almost all the cooking so you're bound to be pleased no matter what you order. No reservations required.

A&W Drive-In and Restaurant is found

at 310 1st Avenue South. Order your meal over a phone, whether inside or out, at this converted drive-in that offers good meals at low prices. A local hangout for seniors because of the good values, you won't be disappointed with their burgers, fish and chips or chicken - all for well under $5.00, including a drink. Locals like the Coney Dogs on special every Tuesday and the good service from local high schools kids. Of course, the root beer and soft ice cream are a great treat.

Hardee's and Burger King are both represented in town should your tastes run to genuinely predictable fare. Both are located just off the interstate.

Happy Gardens is four blocks west of the underpass at 409 W. Main, phone 628-8268. Thought by many to be the finest Chinese restaurant in the area, the food is excellent, beer and wine is available and the service is first-rate. Good choices are Sizzling Beef or Sam See Chicken if your taste buds like to be fired up. Great daily lunch special that includes soup, egg roll and main course for $3.95. Wor Mein noodles are always a joy. Regular patrons include many who travel long distances to enjoy the excellent dishes prepared with skill and loving care.

> **"Good Choices Are Sizzling Beef Or Sam See Chicken"**
>
> **Happy Gardens Restaurant**

A great picnic spot is Riverside Park and Campground just south of the river on US 310/212 only 2 miles from downtown Laurel. Picnic tables, restrooms, large cottonwoods and lots of room to park make this a pleasant place to stop. Fireman's Park is right downtown at the corner of First Avenue and Main Street and offers picnic tables and an easy walk to many downtown shops.

The Senior Citizens' Center is found at 420 South 4th Avenue, phone 628-7571. A great lunch is served daily to seniors between 12-1 when about 30 eat cafeteria style for only $1.25 each. Visitors welcome, but please call ahead a day in advance.

Laurel's service clubs welcome visitors. The Rotary Club meets every Tuesday at 12:15 p.m. in the basement of the United Methodist Church at 3rd Ave and 4th Street with exceptional family style lunch available for $5.00. Kiwanis meets each Wednesday morning for breakfast at 7 at the Owl Diner, 203 E. Main Street where the small group orders off the menu. Lions Club meets at the Locomotive Inn at 7 for a dinner meeting on the 2nd Tuesday of each month.

WHERE TO STAY

Best Western Locomotive Inn at 310 First Avenue South, phone 628-8281, is a nice 51 unit motel offering indoor pool, hot tub, sauna and non-smoking rooms. Restaurant and lounge are next door and many rates under $50. Managers Roland and Joyce Bratland are longtime residents of Laurel and a great source of information on the area.

Russell Motel is situated at 711 E. Main Street, phone 628-6513. This very clean, well-kept 15 unit, single-level motel has some kitchenettes available and is an easy walk to the Railside Diner. You wont find more accommodating hosts than managers John and Patsy Rosenberg.

City-operated Riverside Park Campground facility is one mile south of I-90 off Exit #434 on US 310-212 road to Red Lodge and offers 7 spaces with electric hook-ups and water, no sewer spaces at $7/night and 40 spaces with no services at $5/night. Showers and restrooms are available May through Oct. Caretaker Herb Mohs available at 628-2491. This clean facility is nestled in towering cottonwoods along banks of the Yellowstone River. Nearest private campground is in Billings.

WHERE TO SHOP

Ye Olde Curiosity Shoppe, 103 East Main, phone 628-7146 is open 10-5 Mon.-Sat. and offers a large selection of

"Ask Velda About The Time She Danced With Fred Astaire"

Ye Olde Curiosity Shoppe

jewelry with many one-of-a-kind items. Good collection of vintage clothing and hats. If you see owner Velda Thomas, ask her about her days as an entertainer in Florida, her celebrity gowns and the time she danced with Fred Astaire.

Bonnies Antiques at 1009 E. Main Street presents a nice selection of furniture and collectibles in a clean, uncluttered setting.

Van Bebber Rock Shop is operated by a long-time rock hound and is located at 207 W. Main, phone 628-4594. Hours are 8:30-5:30 Mon.-Sat. Good selection of Montana agate, fossils, crystals and jewelry, with some antiques. Mrs. Van Bebber has lots of information for rock hounds and appointments for after-hour showings are available.

Mountain Meadowlark Gallery and Frame Shop is found at 101 E. Main, phone 628-8575 and hours are 9-5:30 Mon.-Sat. See Description in

Display/Exhibit classification. Good Selection of art.

Brown's Shell Shack Guns and Pawn is at 113 E. Main, phone 628-8986 and hours are 9:30-5 Mon.-Sat. Good selection of used and new guns with interesting display of mounts and extensive inventory of outdoor supply items. Tom has hunted and fished in this area for many years and is a knowledgeable source for information about local gun dealers. When you see Tom, ask him how big that trout was he held up for a picture in the Custer Country Guide.

LeDuc Jewelry at 13 1/2 Colorado, 628-4817, is a unique shop offering hand-crafted silver and gold jewelry by Kate Stevenson, a local goldsmith trained in Europe. Newest addition is hand made dolls that will charm you. Frequently in the shop and available for showings after hours, Kate operates store with husband Sandy, a native of Scotland. If you meet Sandy, you'll enjoy his heavy Scottish brogue and his strong opinions about everything.

"Handmade Dolls Will Charm You"

LeDuc Jewelry

WATERING HOLES

Caboose Saloon is located at 704 W. Main. Nicely done, the rustic facility has a great backbar, an excellent collection of Bill Rains sculptures and the only live music in town. Country western bands usually liven up the place on weekends, and owner/operator Terry Fink will always have a big smile if you meet him. Lots of Poker and Keno machines available.

Curt's Saloon is found at 220 1st Avenue South, phone 628-8241. Steaks and burgers are also available in this nicely finished extension of Little Big Man Pizza restaurant. Ask owner/operators Curt and Francie Riemann about their annual Beaver Feed but don't make bartender Phil tell you how much time he spends in the water when rafting down the Stillwater.

Locomotive Inn Casino at 216 First Avenue South, phone 628-7969, is located next to Locomotive Inn Motel. Decor is great and the atmosphere cozy in both gaming room and bar. Good selection of food available from restaurant.

Palace Bar & Lanes is found in downtown Laurel at 305 Main, 628-8788. Popular after-work hangout for many locals, the newly remodeled Palace has lots of machines for gaming and the only live Keno in town. Owner Darrell McGillen is chief of the highly respected local volunteer fire department, but if you meet him, don't knock the Bears or the Cubs.

Sid's Place is located 1/2 mile east of

town on Main Street, phone 628-8946. Completely remodeled, Sid's sports Laurel's only volleyball court and serves a great 'Porkie' sandwich. Many locals love the finger steaks and owner/operator Randy Peers still operates the kitchen like a roadhouse.

EXHIBITS AND DISPLAYS

Mountain Meadowlark Gallery and Frame Shop is located at 101 E. Main St., phone 628-8575. Hours are 9-5:30 Mon.-Sat. and owners Marylee Moreland and Gary Temple have a good display of original and limited edition art. Marylee is an accomplished painter and sculptor and Gary's metalwork is becoming widely known in the region. Specializing in western art, the shop offers collectibles, fine art and memorabilia in a comfortable setting. If Gary's there, be sure to ask about his truly unique mailboxes, but avoid talking about diets—he can't stay away from the pasta with white sauce.

> **"Marylee's Latest Piece Will Wow You"**
>
> **Mountain Meadowlark Gallery**

Oscar's Dreamland is at the south end of Shiloh Road half way between Billings and Laurel, phone 656-0966, hours are seasonal. The fifteen acre park boasts a large display of antique farm equipment and artifacts. Of particular note is the 500-piece collection of steam, gasoline and horse drawn machinery, much of which is still in operating condition. Although Oscar's daughter Marcie Ann runs the attraction, Owner Oscar Cooke visits the park regularly even though he's near his 90's. If you see him, ask about the time he filled an entire train full of farm equipment he sold in the 30's.

Sonny O'Days Bar and Boxing Hall of Fame is located at 209 East Main Street. A unique bar operated by one time welterweight contender, dubbed the "Kid from Meaderville" because of his roots in Butte MT. Walls feature over 1000 autographed pictures, posters and other memorabilia collected from national notables. If you meet Sonny, you won't soon forget him.

Ray's Taxidermy is just south of the Yellowstone River on US 310/212, phone 628-7656. Nice display of life size mounts with many hides and skulls for sale. Specializing in fish mounts, owner Ray Hatfield knows the backcountry of southern Montana as well as anyone in the area and is an avid fisherman/hunter. If you have a chance, ask him about the buffalo hides available due to "harvest" of animals that came out of Yellowstone Park.

HISTORIC PLACES

Canyon Creek Battlefield is located 7 miles north of Laurel. An historical marker identifies the site of this famous battle between the retreating Nez Perce Indians under Chief Joseph as they eluded the 7th Calvary in Sept. 1887. More information is available at the Mountain Meadowlark Gallery, 101 E. Main. A painting depicting battle can be viewed in the Yellowstone Bank lobby, 12 First Ave.

Calamity Jane's Horse Cache is also situated 7 miles north of Laurel just west of the Canyon Creek Battlefield marker. This is where this frontier character, muleskinner, gambler and lady of the night called home for a time in the late 1800's. The butte was used to corral horses owned by "Calamity" Jane Canary, as only one access point needed to be fenced. For more information, contact Gary at Mountain Meadowlark Gallery.

RECREATION

Laurel Golf Club is located west of Laurel, phone 628-4504. Excellent 18 hole private course with grass greens and is rated in top 10 in Montana. The course is easy to walk and offers challenging play with lots of water and interesting layout. Good food in the public restaurant, but check on limited seasonal hours. Reciprocal golf available year round to card carrying members of any USGA-affiliated club more than 50 miles away. Tee times available one week in advance only. Weekends are very busy.

"Rated In Montana's Top Ten"

Laurel Golf Club

Fishing is good with great access to the Yellowstone River at both Riverside Park south of town on US 212/310 or west at Sportsman's Park. Easy 3 hour float from Sportsman's to the Fish and Game boat ramp at Riverside. Most locals head south to Rockcreek, west to the Stillwater or over to the Bighorn River for the best fishing in the area. Check with Dean at Coast to Coast or Tom at Brown's Shell Shack for local information and conditions. If you see Dean, ask him how he lost his fishing rod on a trip down the Bighorn with Milt and Kent.

SPECIAL EVENTS

Herbstfest is a very popular three-day festival celebrating Laurel's German heritage. It's held annually on the 4th weekend in September and offers continuous entertainment and food booths through Sunday at the high school, with dancing in the beerstube tent

Friday and Saturday evenings. For details, contact Jean Carroll Thompson at 628-7582 or 628-4508

Fourth of July is a special day in Laurel with the Jaycee street dance the night before kicking off a full day of activities including a Jaycee breakfast in Fireman's Park, kiddie parade at 10, regular parade at 11, Fireman's Bar-B-Q in Thomson Park at noon, Legion Baseball in the afternoon and one of the largest free fireworks displays in the state at dusk.

EMERGENCY INFORMATION

Laurel Exxon Servicecenter is downtown at 201 W. Main, phone 628-4216. Owner/operator Dave Powers has provided locals and tourists with conscientious, economical automotive and RV repair for over 20 years and has mechanic on duty 8-6 Mon.-Sat. For emergency after-hour service, call Laurel Police at 628-8737. AAA towing is provided in Laurel by Mike Penne at Modern Auto Wrecker Service, phone 628-7145.

Laurel Medical Center at 1035 First Avenue, phone 628-6311, has four doctors on duty during office hours, 8-5 Mon.-Fri. and 8-12 Sat. Get emergency after-hour assistance by contacting doctor on duty using same phone number. Nearest emergency room in Billings.

Beartooth Veterinary Clinic can take good care of your pet at 419 E. Main St., phone 628-4309. Extensive experience with small and large animal practice qualifies owner Dr. Krayton Kerns as a reliable and caring Vet. Regular office hours are 8-5 Mon-Fri and 8-12 Sat; after hours use same number to contact Vet on duty.

LEWISTOWN

Lewistown is located in the geographic center of Montana. The county seat of Fergus County, agriculture is the primary industry, although gold mining has created new employment in recent years. The community is surrounded by four mountain ranges and the beautiful Spring Creek flows right through town. A great local resource is the city water that's spring generated and doesn't see daylight until it comes out of the tap. The town has numerous buildings listed on the Historical Register, many of which are included in an interesting walking tour you can find out about at the museum or your motel.

> **"Specialties Include Spanish Omelet With Fresh Salsa"**
>
> **Sportsman's Restaurant**

The community sports a new high school, city complex, county complex, hospital and town convention center, all built with locally raised taxes and donations. Tourist information can be found in the Central Montana Museum Building on the east side of town at 408 NE Main. Hours are 9-12 and 1:30-5 Mon-Fri, phone is 538-5436 and contact person is Webb Brown.

WHERE TO EAT

The Whole Famdamily is located at 206 1/2 Main, open 11-8 and operated by Mark and DeeDee Heinert. You'll enjoy the great homemade specials, huge sandwiches and friendly service. Local favorites include the Mexican Special (Friday's Taco Salad with Homemade Salsa is great) and the Beefy Beatrice Sandwich.

Sportsman's Restaurant at 133 Wunderlin is open 7 a.m. till 9 p.m., has handicapped access and lots of seating. Specialties include Spanish Omelet with fresh salsa and Sports Burger with mushrooms and your choice of cheese.

Local Service organizations welcome visitors with noon meeting schedules at the Park Inn for Rotary on Mondays, Kiwanis on Tuesdays and Lions on Thursdays.

WHERE TO STAY

Park Inn (formerly the Yogo Inn) has 100 units and is operated by Henry Gehl. A longtime favorite for travelers and conventioneers, it's recently been redecorated and offers indoor pool, restaurant & bar and gift shop that will make your stay enjoyable. Phone 538-8721 for reservations or more information.

Spring Creek Bed & Breakfast is operated by Ernie and Bev Fachner on the upper Spring Creek and offers a peaceful, out of the way stopping off point where wildlife literally comes right to your door. Call 538-9768 for details or reservations.

"Wildlife Right At Your Door"

Spring Creek Bed and Breakfast

Circle Bar Guest Ranch located in Utica is a true Montana dude ranch and is owned and operated by Sarah Hollatz. Located near sapphire mines in the beautiful mountains on the Judith River, you won't find better hospitality. When you meet Sarah, be sure to ask her about "What the Hay."

SHOPPING

Country Junction at 216 W. Main is operated by Jenny Gehl and loaded with wonderful gifts, gourmet coffees, teas and made in Montana items. If you get to meet Jenny, inquire about "A Touch of Class."

Don's Store is located at the corner of Janeaux and 2nd Ave. and is run by Dale Pfau. It's a great place to find western goods, Yogo Sapphire jewelry and a valuable contact point for sports enthusiasts, especially hunting and fishing buffs.

Antique Acres in Hwy 19 at the Fairgrounds Road is operated by Jerry and Evelyn Bussy and offers something for every antique lover. Call 538-5194 for hours and directions.

WATERING HOLES

4 Aces Casino at 508 First Ave. N. is run by Lonnie Bergstrom and home of the giant chicken fried steak (a half is really plenty).

Eagles Club at 124 W. Main is run by John Southworth and has great weekend bands for dancing (usually country western).

EXHIBITS

Central Montana Museum has a great selection of historical items from central Montana, is located at 408 NE Main and is open 8-12 and 1:30-5.

Lewistown Art Center at 801 W. Broadway is open 1-5 daily except Sunday and Monday and features a good selection of art by regional and local artists. You'll definitely enjoy the gift shop offering jewelry, pottery and prints for sale.

HISTORIC PLACES

Kendall and Maiden Canyon are old gold mining towns with good picnic areas nearby. Details are available from the Chamber.

RECREATION

Lewistown Elks Golf Club is located on Country Club Road southeast of town and is one of Montana's best nine-hole courses with lots of trees and hilly, undulating fairways. Semiprivate club rules state visitors living more than 30 miles away are always welcome. Call 538-7075 for a tee time.

The Fish Hatchery on upper Spring Creek is an interesting stop and offers a picnic area and free tours of the trout hatchery from 8-5. Fishing access is available, too.

SPECIAL EVENTS

Chokecherry Festival is an annual event in Lewistown celebrating the harvest of this distinctly Montana fruit, featuring a parade, foot race, play and dance. Call the Chamber for details at 538-5436.

EMERGENCY INFORMATION

You won't be disappointed by the service at Dean Newton Olds, Cadillac, GMC. Owner Dean Newton has a downtown location at 514 W. Broadway and an extremely helpful staff. Regular hours are 8-5 and phone is 538-3455.

Central Montana Hospital is located at 408 Wendell Ave and offers 24 hours care by calling 538-7711 or 911.

Lewistown Veterinary Service on Fairgrounds Road can take care of any pet problems. Dr. Raths and Dr. Walters are good with both small and large animals and can be reached at 538-3663, 9-5 Mon.-Sat.

LOLO

Lolo, 8 miles south of Missoula on Highway 93, is at the entrance to the Bitterroot Valley, one of the most picturesque garden spots of western Montana. Considered a bedroom community for Missoula by many, Lolo is a town of approximately 5000 residents. Sitting at the junction of Hwy 93 and US 12 West serving Montana and Idaho, the small commercial district includes a bank, grocery store, three convenience stores, hardware outlet, art gallery, medical/dental facility and several bars and restaurants. Lolo locals are typically outspoken and take great pride in their schools. A popular local attraction is the Lolo Hot Springs located 25 miles up Lolo Creek on US 12. Tourist information is available from local merchants, who you'll find both friendly and anxious to help.

WHERE TO EAT

Guy's Lolo Creek Steak House is located at 6600 US 12. This exceptional facility operated by Guy and Whitney Leibenguth is open everyday except Monday and will give you an unforgettable dining experience as you watch your steak cooked over a wood fired grill. Great atmosphere, and you can't miss with the Lolo Steak or Peel and Eat Shrimp. Call 273-2622 for reservations.

"Watch Your Steak Cooked Over A Wood Fired Grill"

Guy's Lolo Creek Steak House

Piney Woods is just up Lolo Creek from the turnoff on US 12 and is a good place for large portions of great food. Arlan and Lorraine Fries are owners/operators and serve some of the best breakfasts and lunches around.

King's Hat at 104 Glacier on the east end of town is a favorite for many locals and run by Arnold, Helen, Larry and Gary Jarvie. Hamburgers are especially good and they offer a special Roscoe Salad that is really a burrito covered with lettuce, cheese, tomatoes, sour cream or blue cheese dressing and topped with homemade chili! This one you won't forget.

P.J.'s Pizza and Pasta at 6555 US 12 is run by Paul Watling, offers a good salad bar and pizza special daily for lunch. Locals like the great bread sticks with pizza, lasagna or spaghetti. Paul delivers during the day, so if the place is locked, just wait a minute for him to come back....it's worth it.

Great picnicking can be had at Fort Fizzle about 3 miles up picturesque Lolo Creek on US 12. This is the spot where Chief Joseph outmaneuvered a group of volunteers brought up from Fort Missoula on his great retreat of 1877. No remnants of the fort exist, but the scenery is super.

WHERE TO STAY

Lolo Hot Springs is located on US 12 about 25 miles west of the junction at Lolo. Ken Hansen offers great camping sites and a motel with 18 units, restaurant and natural hot springs swimming pool. Great stopping off place. Call 273-2290 for details.

Afton's Square Dancing Center at 9955 US 12 has camp hookups and an interesting store specializing in square dance accessories. Afton Granger can give directions and details at 273-0141.

SHOPPING

Thistle Dew Antiques about 10 miles up US 12 has a nice selection and is run by Roy and Stella Van Ostrand. Call 273-6766 for hours and details.

Lolo True Value is located in the Lolo Shopping Center and run by Jim and Cindy Sellers. Along with hardware, auto parts and rentals, Jim and Cindy can fill you in on what's going on in the area and where to go to catch the big one.

Heritage Gallery in the Shopping Center offers a good selection of local and Southwestern art. See Exhibits.

WATERING HOLES

Roadrunner Bar in the Shopping Center offers good food, honest drinks and lots of gaming machines.

KT's Hayloft Saloon and Deli at 11885 S. US 93 is run by Sherrie Medlen and offers a good special everyday.

EXHIBITS

Heritage Gallery in the Lolo Shopping Center is owned and operated by Pat and Linda Holt and open 10-6 Tues-Sat. This one will please you as it's known as one of the finest galleries in Western Montana and offers a good selection both local and Southwestern art. Phone is 273-2404.

Fort Fizzle, situated three miles up US 12 west of Lolo, is the spot where Chief Joseph outsmarted the U.S. military one more time in his escape from an unwanted war. His ability to stay ahead of a strong and mobile U.S. Army force while bringing over 800 men, women and children through the heavily forested Lolo Valley and over the Lolo Pass is a good example of strength of this extraordinary band of non-treaty Nez Perce Indians. From this point Joseph went south down the Bitterroot Valley; he surrendered just a few miles from Canada in north central Montana.

RECREATION

Bitterroot River and Lolo Creek offer outstanding fishing with many accesses near town.

EMERGENCY INFORMATION

Your car will be treated well at Windy's Auto Repair. Jim can be reached at 273-6420 or at 2 Nightingale Place.

Lolo Family Practice located at 11350 S. US 93 has regular office hours from 8:30-5, phone 273-0045. Either Dr. Ned Vasquez or Dr. Judy Visscher seem always available. Nearest emergency facilities are in Missoula, 10 minutes away.

Lolo Creek Veterinary Hospital is located at 9825 S. US 93 and is open 8-5 Mon.-Fri. and 9-1 on Sat. Phone 273-6335 for appointment or in case of emergency.

MALTA

Located at the crossroads of US 2, US 191 and Montana 242 north to Canada, Malta offers great western hospitality. The community is the center of a large trade area that draws business from all over north central Montana and nearby Canada. It has good facilities, 250 well stocked businesses and a friendly population willing to help visitors make the most out of their vacations. Malta is the seat of Phillips County, lies on the Milk River sixty five miles south of the mighty Missouri and the CM Russell Wildlife Refuge first explored by Lewis and Clark in the early 1800's. Home to both the Bowdoin and CMR Wildlife Refuges, Phillips county offers great diversity of wildlife viewing, hunting or fishing. Fifty miles south of town you'll find the Little Rockies, a mountainous upthrust know for its gold and silver mining history. Tourist information can be found in the Chamber of Commerce sponsored racks at the Westside Sporting Goods Store, or by calling Anne Boothe at 654-1776.

> **"Locals Like The Super Sandwich"**
>
> **L & L Country Deli**

WHERE TO EAT

L & L Meats and Country Deli at 205 North 1st East has a cozy, down-home atmosphere and offers great food. The place is owned and operated by Leonard and Linda Mingneau and locals like to order a Super Sandwich, great homemade soups or Linda's special salads.

Westside Restaurant on Highway 2 west of town is operated by Inga Baumgartner and is a popular spot with the locals who frequently gather to drink coffee and solve a few world problems. You'll really enjoy the salad bar and the beef is great, no matter how it's fixed.

WHERE TO STAY

GN Motor Hotel at 2 South and 1st East has 29 units and is operated by Kay and Dale. Facility offers dining room, lounge, steak house, coffee shop, banquet and convention rooms, inside parking and cable TV. Call 654-2100 for reservations.

Sportsman's Motel at 231 North 1st St. on Hwy 2 has 13 units. Owners Dan and Lou Lundstrom cater to the sportsman, always aim to please and love to visit about what's going on around town. If you see Dan, ask him about the great Elk hunting in Phillips county. Phone is 654-2300.

Edgewater Hotel and Trailer Court is on Hwy 2 west of town. Modern 32 unit operation is run by Lee and Jim Knudsen and offers sauna, jacuzzi, pool, weight room and location right on the Milk River. If you get to meet Lee, he'll be happy to fill you in on what's happening around Phillips County.

SHOPPING

MJ's Trading Post at 101 S. 1st Ave. is owned and operated by Mike Carney and one of Malta's first stores offering men's and women's western wear. Featuring authentic store displays from the 1880's, it's a real showplace and if you see Mike, be sure to ask him about the history of Edwards and McCellan.

Koss Kollection at 26 S. 1st E. is owned and operated by Sandy and Dorene Koss. The two sisters have teamed up to create one of the most interesting and accommodating hardware stores you'll ever see. Visitors enjoy crafts by locals artists and a special antique display. If you see Dorene, ask her for a story or two about what it was like living in the desolate Missouri breaks 50 miles south of Malta.

WATERING HOLES

Roger's Saloon and Chuckwagon at 147 S. 1st Ave. E. in downtown Malta is run by Byron Freaux and Bob Murphy and offers great dancing to the music of Montana's own Randy Rhoads and his classic country band. If you see Linda, be sure to ask her why the bow tie.

Stockman Bar is owned by Lyle Mayhew and is a classic Montana establishment. If you see Lyle, he'll be glad to give you the history of the bar and a look at a hidden painting by William Standing.

"Store Displays From The 1880's"

MJ's Trading Post

Mustang Lanes and Casino at 122 S. 1st Ave. E. is run by Jim and Regina Ereaux and offers great pizza, bowling, Vegas-style Casino and even rollerskating. A popular place for great family entertainment.

EXHIBITS

Hi Line Art Gallery and Frame on Hwy 2 East is owned by artist Judy Michail and offers good selection of art in nice setting. Phone Judy at 654-1551 for hours and details about what's on display.

Phillips County Museum at 133 S. 1st West is open from 10-12 and 1-5 Tues.-Sat. from Memorial Day to Labor Day. Manager Sally Schumacher can be reached at 654-1037 and offers interesting exhibits displaying weapons from Civil War days, Indian artifacts including native American buckskin dresses and beadwork, pelts from timber wolves, brown bear, saddles and many old photographs.

"Native American Buckskin Dresses"

Phillips County Museum

HISTORIC PLACES

Buffalo jumps and historic native American village sites are numerous and can be located through the Bureau of Land Management office in town. Contact Bonnie Wiederrick at 654-1240 for directions and some experiences you won't soon forget.

Zortman Landusky Historic Mining Town is located 48 miles south of Malta, 7 miles off of US 191. Contact David Rummel for information at 654-3559, write Box 405, Zortman, MT 59546, or just enjoy the get away to picturesque Zortman. Hidden in the Little Rock Mountains, you can experience panning for gold, a unique place to camp with good fishing and backpacking nearby or a comfortable stay in the rustic, yet modern, cabins after a tour of the Zortman Landusky Mine.

RECREATION

Sleeping Buffalo is 17 miles E. and one mile north of Malta. Enjoy a stay in one of 17 rustic cabins and soak in any of the three mineral pools (two are indoors). Facility has 9 hole golf course, 70 RV hookups, waterslide with fishing and boating only a mile away at the Nelson Reservoir. Facility has large enclosed picnic area with horseshoe

"Tour The Zortman Landusky Mine"

48 Miles South of Malta

pits, baseball fields and three volleyball courts. Outstanding for family reunions or overnight stop. Phone 527-3370 for the lowdown or a reservation.

Marion Hills Country Club at 100 Doral Land is south of Malta on 191. Large grass greens, wide rolling fairways and three tee areas per hole make this an exciting and challenging golf course. Call 654-1648 for a tee time.

SPECIAL EVENTS

Milk River Wagon Train is a great local event that takes a different route each year. Call Dixon Grant at 654-1336 for details on how to take advantage of this opportunity to recreate old west travel. Riders and wagons travel along the prairie, camping under the stars at night after enjoying old time dancing, music and Bar-B-Q. Wagon Train destination is Malta and the annual Labor Day Parade.

Phillips County Fair is held 17 miles west of town in Dodson just off Highway 2. The event provides an annual showcase for the work of hundreds of adult and 4-H participants. Ranch-style rodeo features pony, horse and chuckwagon races, ranch roundup, craft and cooking displays, games, carnival rides and demolition derby. If you've never seen one, this kind of county fair is something you really shouldn't miss.

EMERGENCY INFORMATION

Delta Ford at 102 S. 1st Ave. will service your car without a hassle. Owners Larry Matthews and Ben Browder have a mechanic on duty 8-5 Mon.-Fri. and 9-12 on Sat. but call 654-1850 for help anytime. Wrecker service available also.

Phillips County Family Health Clinic and Hospital, 315 S. 8th E. can help with medical problems 24 hours a day. Clinic phone is 654-1800 and hours are 9-5. Hospital is located at 417 S. 4th St. E. and phone is 654-1100. Call the sheriff at 654-1211 if you need help getting to fully-equipped emergency room.

Your pet will be treated well at the Phillips County Veterinary Clinic located 2 miles south of town on Highway 191, phone 654-1794. The clinic has great facilities and boards large and small animals.

MEDICINE LAKE

Medicine Lake is a friendly little town of 350 people located in northeastern Montana approximately 2 hours north of Glendive off I-94 on Highway 16 and on the way to Regina, Sask. The town is one mile north of Medicine Lake and the Medicine Lake National Wildlife refuge offering close to 30,000 acres of lakes, prairies, coulees and wilderness with hundreds of bird species and wildlife. Hunting is a favorite pastime of area residents and area offers some of the best pheasant hunting anywhere. Farming and ranching are the primary sources of income in the area and Sheridan Electric Cooperative is the largest employer, taking care of electrical needs for a three county area. Travelers won't be disappointed as the community offers a full line of services and many good restaurants. The town park is a good place to stop and enjoy the peace and quiet while you watch the kids swim, play a little golf at the parks 4-hole course or pick up on a little action at the horseshoe pits. Tourist information is available at Hustslar's Hardware Store from local commercial club officer Tim Hutslar or from Wayne Hendrickson at the local Credit Union. The Medicine Lake Refuge is open 7-4 and manager Ted Gutzke can even provide a guide by calling 789-2305.

WHERE TO EAT

Lake Cafe on Main Street is open 5 a.m. to 7 p.m. and has great home cooked meals and pastries. Owner Janice Melton opens early everyday and serves super breakfasts for hunters. Locals like the daily specials, fresh rolls, pies and Janice's special Laketonian Burger.

If you like to picnic, the Medicine Lake Wildlife Refuge is a good spot with

"Great Picnic Spot"

Medicine Lake Wildlife Refuge

tables and BBQ grills. The city park also has grills, tables and is a pleasant place to stop.

WHERE TO STAY

Joyce's Bed & Breakfast at 604 Minnehan in the southeast part of town has two beds available and serves great breakfasts. Owner Joyce Cooper can be reached at 789-2421 for more information.

Club Bar and Hotel at 210 Main Street has 4 units. Owner Danny Olson is known as "Radar" and serves great homemade pizza and has good drinks and popular gaming machines. Call 789-2208 for reservations.

Stringer's Camper Hookups northwest of town has parking and electricity hookups for RV's during the summer and fall months. Good spot for hunters to stay and owner Wayne Stringer is always willing to share information on where the action is. Call 789-2244 for more information.

SHOPPING

Hutslar's Hardware at 208 Main is open 8:30 till 5:30 and features "Big Spring Water," hardware and the State Liquor Store. If you get to meet owner Tim Hutslar, be sure to ask about his antiques and tractor collection.

Lake Ag Supply and Variety Store at 220 Main is open 8-5:30 and owners Roger and Larae Krumwiede offer a little bit of everything including sporting goods and advice on where to find the best in outdoor recreation in the area.

Jack and Jill Store has the grocery item you're looking for and is open 8:30-5:30 Monday through Saturday. If owner George Waters Jr. is around, ask for a great story about goose hunting, he's got plenty.

WATERING HOLES

Eight Ball Bar at 209 Main is open at 10 daily and offers daily lunch specials in the bar and lounge owned by Gerald Jensen. This local sports club has large screen TV and if you see J.J., ask him why the Broasted Chicken is so popular.

Club Bar and Hotel at 210 Main Street has good drinks and lots of gaming machines. You'll never be disappointed by "Radar's" great homemade pizza.

EXHIBITS

Hutslar's Hardware at 208 Main has a good selection of antiques from the area and an interesting miniature tractor collection. Open 8:30-5:30 and run by Tim Hutslar.

RECREATION

Medicine Lake National Wildlife Refuge is located one mile south of town and is open 7-4 daily. Manager Ted Gutzke can be reached at 789-2305. The refuge was built in the 1930's during the Great Depression. The area was declared a National Wilderness Area in 1976 and is home to hundreds of species of birds and other upland game. Roads are maintained and allow visitors great viewing of the very special attraction. Paths are available for hiking also.

Pheasant Hunting around Medicine Lake is the best in Montana and hunters from all of the country come to enjoy the sport in the public hunting areas and on private ground with owners' permission. Ted Gutzke at the Refuge is great source of information to get you in on the hunt of a lifetime.

SPECIAL EVENTS

Annual Medicine Lake Bar-B-Que with carnival and street dance is a great local event held the last Saturday in June each year. Highlighted by a BBQ Beef feed and game booths for the kids, live music caps off the evening with a dance in the park. Call Tim Hutslar at 789-2345 for details.

EMERGENCY INFORMATION

Herman Oil at Hwy 16 and Main can help out with mechanical problems. Manager Jerimy Bruhn is usually available 7-10 for assistance, phone is 789-2242.

Sheridan Memorial Hospital and Clinic is located at 440 W. Laurel Avenue in Plentywood. Emergency Medical Technicians are on call in Medicine Lake and the ambulance is just 15 minutes away. Call 765-1234 in case of emergency or go to Plentywood for non-emergency care.

Plentywood Veterinary Clinic is located one mile east of Plentywood, just 20 miles north of Medicine Lake on Hwy 16. Call 765-1760 if your pet needs help.

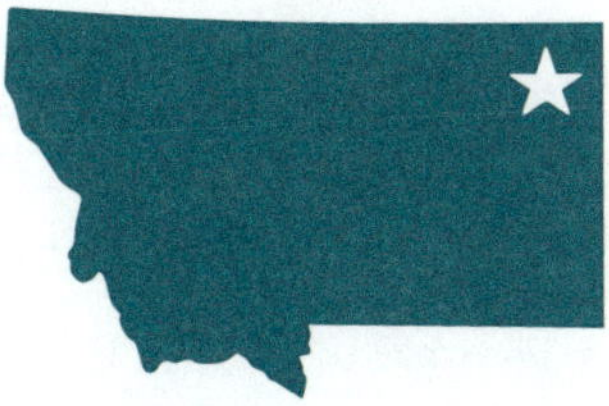

PLENTYWOOD

Plentywood is a high plains community of 2200 people in the northeast corner of the state, just 120 miles south of Regina. You actually have to pass through Plentywood to reach the 24 hour Port of Entry at Regway. Farming and ranching provide the backbone of the local economy with spring and durum wheat most plentiful. With no mountains and little water, the locals know how to create their own fun through local sports, getting together over a good steak or enjoying the great eastern Montana out-of-doors. Tourist information is available at 515 W. 1st Avenue in the lobby of the Sherwood Inn or by contacting Paul Overgaard at 765-2810.

WHERE TO EAT

Blue Moon Night Club east of Plentywood has long been a famous stop in the area. Open 6-12 Tues-Sunday, Mert and Delores Kemmis provide nightly entertainment and a friendly atmosphere in this traditional roadhouse. Whatever you order, you'll enjoy great dining and the small steak, baby sirloin or halibut are highly recommended. Call 765-2491 for a reservation.

Randy's Restaurant at 323 W. 1st Avenue is owned and operated by Randy Matzke and offers great breakfasts and burgers. If you get a chance, ask Randy to tell you why his Randy Burger is so popular.

Alta Vista Cafe is located across from the Sherwood Inn at 564 W. 1st Avenue and opens early for breakfast.

> **"World Famous Supper Club"**
>
> **Blue Moon Night Club**

WHERE TO STAY

Sherwood Inn at 515 W. First Avenue has 69 units, a 24 hour desk, complimentary coffee, laundry facilities, restaurant, lounge and even a beauty shop. If you get to see owner/operator Paul Overgaard, he's a great source of local information about anything and everything. Call for a reservation at 765-2810.

SHOPPING

Hi Line Sports at 558 W. 1st Ave. is open 8-5:30 and offers a complete line of sportswear and equipment for the sportsman. Owner Lowell Young usually has a good joke to share, so if you see him ask for his latest.

Peterson's Men's and Ladies Wear at 112 N. Main has a nice selection of quality clothing. Owner Bill Peterson is an avid golfer and can give you the low-down on the best courses in the area.

Sheridan Floral and Gift at 525 W. 1st Ave. is open 9-5:30, has nice variety of gift, antiques and outstanding selection of fresh and freeze-dried flowers. If you meet owner Marilyn Nelson, ask her to demonstrate her freeze-drying technique.

WATERING HOLES

Robin Hood Lounge is open at 1:00 daily and located at 520 W. Railroad Ave. Owner Paul Overgaard operates the friendly bar, restaurant and casino with a relaxed atmosphere.

Vets Club is operated by PeeWee Robertson and open 1-1. Great place to get an honest drink and meet lots of friendly locals.

Cassidy's Bar and Lounge at 105 S. Main is open at 9 daily. The popular local casino is run by Butch Niesen and offers a lively atmosphere.

EXHIBITS

Sheridan County Museum is located east of town at the entrance to the fairgrounds. Nice selection of turn-of-the-century items, including replicas of stores and businesses, an old tractor club, antique tractors, steam engines and threshing machines. One of the finest collections of its kind in Montana.

> **"Outstanding Selection Of Freeze Dried Flowers"**
>
> **Sheridan Floral and Gift**

HISTORIC PLACES

Sitting Bull Monument is situated east of town at the fairgrounds and is the site of the surrender of Sitting Bull following the defeat of Custer and escape to Canada in 1876.

RECREATION

Plentywood Golf Club is located northwest of town and offers a nine-hole course with grass greens. Attractive and well-maintained course is fun to play. Be sure to call 765-2532 to check on a tee time as the course is closed to the public at certain times on Ladies and Men's Days.

Upland bird hunting around Plentywood in Sheridan County is some of the best in the world. Contact Lowell Young at 765-1522 for help .

SPECIAL EVENTS

Elks Can-Am Balloon Rally is held in Plentywood in Mid-August each year and offers spectacular opportunity to view international hot air ballooning at its best. Contact Mike Hallesy at 765-1033 for details and dates.

The Herald Softball Tournament held in Sportsman's Park on E. Lasater Ave. is sponsored by the Plentywood Herald and offers some of the best U.S. and Canadian fast-pitch softball around. Call the Herald at 765-1150 for details.

EMERGENCY INFORMATION

Plentywood Motor Sales at 201 N. Main is the local Ford Garage, and offers reliable help with your car problems. Owner Mike McCormick has mechanics on duty from 8-5 weekdays and can be reached at 765-1720.

Sheridan County Hospital and Clinic at 440 W. Laurel Ave. has regular office hours from 8-5, phone 765-1501. For 24-hour emergency help, call the hospital at 765-1420 or ambulance at 765-1234.

Plentywood Veterinary Clinic is located east of town and has office 8-5 hours, phone 765-1760. In case of emergency call 765-1569 for reliable help from Dr. Robert Kane.

"Hot Air Ballooning At Its Best"

Elks Can-Am Balloon Rally

POLSON

Polson is situated at the south end of the beautiful Flathead Lake on Highway 93, a popular route to Glacier Park. The largest fresh water lake west of the Mississippi, Flathead offers endless recreation, and Polson is one place where you can enjoy exceptional boating, swimming, fishing, rafting and golfing. The town is located on the Flathead Indian reservation, home of the Salish-Kootennai Tribe that schedules Pow-Wows open to the public each summer. The local economy has been historically based on ranching, farming and timber but tourism is playing a more major role each year. A photographer's and sun worshiper's paradise, the area's glorious sunrises and gorgeous sunsets accent the magnificent Mission Mountains and are enjoyed by all. Polson is truly a great tourist community you will thoroughly enjoy. Tourist information is available from Phyllis Fulkerson at 883-5969 from 10-5 Mon.-Sat.

WHERE TO EAT

Port of Polson Galley is located at 318 Main and offers outstandingly fresh gourmet meals and great desserts. Owners Doug and Karen Martin have wonderful daily specials and always serve large portions with friendly attention to detail. The locals look forward to the Friday Seafood Bowl, and you can't miss with their great hamburgers and famous homemade seasoned potato chips.

The Schiefelbein Haus at 6395 East Shore on Highway 35 offers a bit of Bavaria. Open April 15th till Oct. 1st, it's an outdoor beer garden with entertainment and great German food you won't soon forget. A special event each year is the Summerfest in August fea-

"The Belgian Waffles Are Great"

The Schiefelbein Haus

turing music, dancing and waffle eating contests. You'll love the Belgian Waffles, touted as the world's best.

WHERE TO STAY

KwaTaqNuk, "Where the Water Leaves the Lake" is a 112 unit motel owned and operated by the Salish and Kootenai Indian Tribes at 303 Hwy 93 East. The beautiful new motel has a casino, lounge, indoor and outdoor pools, jacuzzi, gift shops, gallery, and a full service marina. Enjoy the excellent restaurant and the exceptional view of Flathead Lake framed by the Mission Mountains. Call 883-6363 or 1-800-882-6363 for reservations for a room or a wonderful cruise on the Port Polson Princess that leaves regularly throughout the summer from the motel marina.

Hawthorne House, at 304 Third Ave. E., just one block from Hwy 93 and Flathead Lake, is a great bed-and-breakfast operated by Karen Huffine. Six units are available in this two-story English tudor house with seven gables.

"English Tudor House With Seven Gables"

Hawthorne House

Your stay will include a full or continental breakfast with fresh fruit and homemade pastries with your coffee. Contact Karen at 883-2723 for reservations.

Polson KOA Campground is located on Hwy 93 at Irvine Flats Road, phone 883-2151. Owners Steve and Sherry Leicht offer full-service camping with pool, hot tub, game room, kitchens, laundry facilities, hot showers, playground and convenience store. Truly a great camping spot with a super view of the lake and mountains.

SHOPPING

Granny's Gift Gallery located at 208 Main St. is open 9-5:30 Mon.-Sat. Owner Lois Dupuis has a large selection of gifts that include crystal glassware, collectibles and country kitchen items. Nice place to stop and shop.

Three Dog Down is situated 1/4 mile north of Polson on Hwy 93. Owned and operated by Robert Ricketts, it's a goosedown outlet and offers the best in down comforters, pillows, featherbeds, coats and much more. Bob is an accomplished opera singer and accordion-player so don't be surprised if you're serenaded while you shop!

The First Resort is located at 219 Main, open 9-6 Monday-Saturday and operated by Jim Duford. You'll find a great selection of quality, name brand merchandise in a cheerful shop that shares Polson's nautical theme.

WATERING HOLES

South Shore Inn has been a favorite of many for years and is located at the Junction of Highways 93 and 35 on the south entrance to town. Open from 11-2 daily, it's a nice lounge where you can relax on the spacious deck in the summer and take in a most spectacular view of the lake and the Mission Mountains. Don't miss the opportunity to try the great food inside at the China Gate Restaurant. Phone is 883-2553.

Diamond Horseshoe Lounge, at 820 Shoreline Dr. is a popular local hangout where you can boogie to live music all summer long. Great nightspot with a super atmosphere has a large, two level deck with bar that goes right down to a boat dock. If you're hungry, you'll find really outstanding prime rib right next door at the Orchards Landing Restaurant.

> **"Bar Goes Right Down To The Dock"**
>
> The Diamond Horseshoe Lounge

Pondera Bar and Restaurant at 315 Main St. is a family operation that has been in business for over 25 years and is now run by Jim and Tom Jones. Open at 8 daily, you enjoy good gaming, good conversation and great burgers. If you're in doubt about what to order, try a British Burger.

EXHIBITS

The Crow's Nest Gallery at 214 Main Street is open May 15th till Sept. 1st from 10-7 daily. Owner Lou Marchello has one of the foremost displays of art by many Northwest Artists. Subjects include wildlife, western, still life, portraits, modern and landscapes in a variety of media, all displayed among Lou's collection of great antique furnishings. Don't miss this one!

Miracle of America Museum and Polson Flathead Historic Museum are located south of Polson on Hwy 93 and at 802 Main in town. The Miracle Museum is home of the Paul Bunyan Tug Boat. The Historical Museum in town has pioneer displays, steamboat memorabilia and much more.

HISTORIC PLACES

Kerr Dam is located 8 miles southwest of town and situated on the Flathead River about 2 miles downstream. The dam is 204 feet high (54 feet higher than Niagara Falls) and offers an exceptional vista!

National Bison Range is located in Moise, just south of Polson. A self guid-

> **"Outstanding Self-Guided Tour"**
>
> **National Bison Range—Moise**

ed tour from your vehicle is available and allows you to observe bison, elk, deer, antelope, bighorn sheep and many bird species in their natural surroundings. Also a great place for a picnic.

RECREATION

Port Polson Players perform at 8 p.m. Wednesday-Sunday during the months of July and August. Theater at its best, these summer stock players stage their acts in the Polson Performing Arts Center, the former club house at the Polson Golf Club near the south entrance to town. Good fun with reservations available at 883-9212.

Polson Golf Course is one of the nicest 18 hole public courses in the state with mature trees and outstanding views of the lake. Non-members should reserve tee times a day in advance at 883-2440 due to heavy play by tourists in the summer.

Glacier Raft Co. is headquartered at Riverside Park on Hwy 93. Open 10-2 daily, you can schedule an exciting (yet safe) half-day white water float trip on the Flathead River below Kerr Dam. The warm water and beautiful scenery are enhanced by the elegance of eagles and osprey to make this a truly wonderful and unique experience for people of all ages. Call 883-5383 for reservations.

SPECIAL EVENTS

Montana State Fiddlers Contest is held in the Middle School gym in July and attracts exceptional musicians of all ages from a wide area. Visitors will particularly enjoy jam sessions held in local parks and on lawns and sidewalks surrounding the school during the contest.

> **"Artists' Displays, Sidewalk Sales, Fish Calling Contests, Free Fish Barbecue"**
>
> **Great Mack Attack**

The Great Mack Attack is an annual event centered around a fishing derby where the winner gets $2000. Great fun every year on the last weekend in June, even if you just stop in for the weigh-ins. Local artists' displays, food concessions, sidewalk sales, fish calling contests, free fish BBQ and Saturday Night Street Dance all provide super entertainment. Tom Gilmore at Tom's Tackle, 883-5107, can help you with this year's dates or advice on where you can go to catch the big one.

Kerr Country Rodeo is Polson's great annual western event and offers some new fun for those who would like to camp under Montana stars, ride with a wagon train and enjoy chuckwagon food. If you're interested, call 883-5969 for details or just join the locals for one of the best rodeos around. Enjoy the night rodeo on Friday and Saturday, parade on Saturday, and don't miss the Rodeo Cowboy Water Ski tournament that is great fun for all. Call 883-5969 for times and dates.

EMERGENCY INFORMATION

Polson 93 Exxon offers reliable full service seven days a week at 107 2nd Avenue East. Owner Marshall Bjork has a mechanic on duty from 7:30-6 daily and can be reached at 883-4400.

St. Josephs Hospital on Skyline Dr. in Polson offers help 24 hours a day. Office hours are 7 a.m. to 8 p.m. Call 883-5377 for appointments or emergency care.

Your pet will be well taken care of at South Shore Veterinary Service located on Hwy 93 South. Call 883-5229 for help 9-5:30 Mon.-Fri. or 9-12 Sat. Dr. John Peterson is available for emergency help at same number.

ST. IGNATIUS

Nestled in the heart of the Flathead Indian Reservation at the foot of the beautiful Mission Range, St. Ignatius is home to 2500 residents. Located just 45 minutes north of Missoula and some 30 minutes south of Flathead Lake, St. Ignatius is at the center of much of what's great about western Montana. Agriculture, lumber and small business create most of the employment in the area with many visitors attracted by excellent lake, river and stream fishing. Tourist information is available at the St. Ignatius Chamber of Commerce where Stuart Morton will usually be able to assist you at 745-3123 from 7-6, or by stopping at the Lily of the Valley Floral and Gift Shop on Main Street.

WHERE TO EAT

Old-timers' Cafe, operated by Monty and Sue Werdin, is a great small town cafe with lots of good home cooking.

Allentown Restaurant and Lounge, 6 miles north on Hwy 93 is operated by Rick Tamler. A great restaurant in a beautiful setting offering breakfast, lunch and fine dining.

Picnic at the National Bison Range located just west of St. Ignatius where you'll find nice picnic facilities, a self-guided scenic tour and visitors' center.

WHERE TO STAY

Sunset Motel in St Ignatius is owned and operated by Bill Bick and offers good accommodations at 745-3900.

Doug Allard's Lodge Pole Motel is a good stopping off point next to a very interesting trading post and museum. Call 754-2951 for reservations or information.

Allentown Motel six miles north of St. Ignatius has nice, clean units adjoining great eating at Allentown Restaurant and Lounge. Phone is 745-2951.

EXHIBITS

National Bison Range is located just west of St. Ignatius and is must see.

View western Montana wildlife in natural surroundings.

Four Winds Trading Post, 4 miles north of town on Hwy 93, offers visitors good look at historic buildings and Indian artifacts displayed by Preston Miller.

HISTORIC PLACES

St. Ignatius Catholic Mission offers a great look at early Montana history and is well known for its beautiful art work and sculptures. Built in the early 1800's, the mission offers interesting aspects of early Indian and white settlers' lives and is an enjoyable stop on your way through the Mission Valley.

> **"Beautiful Artwork"**
>
> **St. Ignatius Catholic Mission**

Doug Allard's Flathead Indian Museum and Trading Post is open 8-6 and offers visitors a good look at Indian artifacts, local history and even a close-up view of live Bison in a corral outside. Good browsing in the gift shop and convenience store that often offer locally produced fruit and jelly.

RECREATION

The area offers many lakes, rivers, streams and a wide variety of excellent fishing. Mountain trails for hiking and camping and two golf courses are close by also.

SPECIAL EVENTS

St. Ignatius Good Ol' Days is a two-day celebration held the last weekend of July. Event features games, Bar-B-Q, talent show, street dance and one of the largest small-town parades in the area.

Pioneer Days are held in Ronan, 14 miles north of St. Ignatius, on the first weekend in August. The fun includes a rodeo, games, parade and demolition derby.

EMERGENCY INFORMATION

Stuart's Servicenter is open 8:30-5:30 and operated by Stuart Morton. Stuart will treat you and your pocketbook right and can be reached at 745-2190.

Mission Valley Health Service in Ronan, 14 miles north, can help with medical problems. Call 745-2781 from 8-5, or 676-4441 for emergency assistance.

Castor Veterinary Clinic in St. Ignatius can take care of your pet 8-5. Call 745-2473.

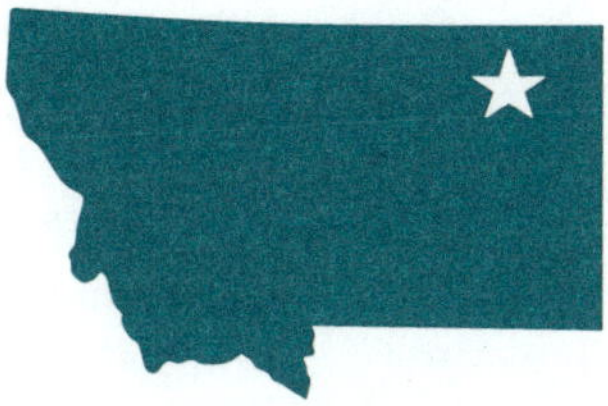

SCOBEY

Scobey is a bustling, friendly little town 48 miles north of Highway 2, situated 14 south of Canada and called the gateway to Saskatchewan. Grain and livestock are king when it comes to income and employment, although tourists are finding the restored Pioneer Town with over 40 structures and museum a very interesting attraction. Tours are available Memorial Day through September. If you're in town over the 4th of July weekend, be prepared for some serious fun. If you prefer a little culture, attend the ever expanding art show and if you are a history buff, the Pioneer Town Tour and Museum will suit you just fine. Local events include the famous Dirty Same Show featuring the illustrious Dirty Shame Belles, Dixie Land Jazz Band and other great local talent. Feast on the sausage and pancake breakfast in one of the old cook cars and if down right fun sounds good, attend the hilarious "outhouse races" and KCGM's talent contest called the Country Showdown held on Scobey's main street. Local recreation includes a challenging nine hole golf course with grass greens and great bird hunting every fall. Travel accommodations are good and great food is no problem when you can sink your teeth into a steak at the 4 Buttes Supper Club located near the edge of the world where you can get to know the locals and hear about the good ol' days "where the west begins." Tourist information is available at the Daniels County Library and Chamber Information Center, 203 Timmons. Contact Pat or Marlene from 9-5 at 487-5502, Mon.-Fri. for personal assistance.

WHERE TO EAT

Burger Hut on Hwy 13 S. of Scobey is open 11-10 daily and offers great burgers and scrumptious soft ice cream served by car hops. Locals like owners' Patty and Pat's Pizza burgers and chicken, although you'll never be disappointed by Tim's Ugly Burger.

Cozy Cafe at 15 Main St. is a good family restaurant operated by Robert Sanden and offers excellent Chinese food, American dishes and great daily specials. Good bets are the sweet and sour pork or chicken fried steak. If you like Thai food and get to see Kuan, ask about the very special spicy dishes that are available but not on the menu.

Shu Mei's Kitchen is located at 506 1st Ave E. and has good American and Chinese food and great service. Locals come back time and again for owner Shu Mei Swenson's great sauteed shrimp with vegetables and cashew chicken with vegetables.

"Great Sauteed Shrimp With Vegetables"

Shu Mei's Kitchen

Silver Slipper Supper Club on Hwy 13 South is open 11 a.m. to 1:30 p.m. for lunch Mon.-Fri. and 5-12 for dinner everyday except Mondays. Manager Bonnie Meyer creates a great atmosphere and guests enjoy outstanding homemade soups, salads and sandwiches for lunch, and super broasted chicken and pizza for dinner. The chicken is really special (it's cooked from fresh - not frozen) and locals drive for miles to enjoy "Chicken and Jos" at the Silver Slipper. If you see Charlie, ask him anything...he loves to visit.

WHERE TO STAY

Cattle King Motor Inn on Hwy 13 South has 29 units with queen sized beds, handicapped room, cable TV and supper club across the street. Owner Jim Crandell is always anxious to please and if you meet him, ask about his latest hunting or fishing exploit.

SHOPPING

Frames and Things, at 105 Main St., is open 9:30-5:30 Mon.-Sat. Owner Mary Richardson has nice gallery of original art, good selection of Montana-made gifts and specializes in preservation techniques for three dimensional objects. If you are a history buff and get to see Mary or Edgar, be sure to ask about the Daniels County Museum or general information about the area.

Service Drug at 110 Main is drug store operated by Bob Haugo. It has just about anything you'll need to make your stay in Scobey a pleasant one,

"Locals Drive For Miles To Enjoy Chicken And Jo's"

Silver Slipper Supper Club

including a nice section of souvenirs and gift items. Bob is an avid hunter and always willing to share a story.

The Cromwell Convenience Store at the corner of Railroad and Main is a great place to grab a quick sandwich, slice of pizza or homemade caramel roll while Myra or Cary fill you in on the latest local fishing story.

WATERING HOLES

Ponderosa Bar and Pizza at 102 Main is open 11-11 daily. Kyle Myhre operates the place that's known for friendly atmosphere and good drinks. Cafe boasts good food at reasonable prices with best pizza around.

Banjo's Club 109 Bar & Casino at 109 Main is owned and operated by Banjo Girard, and has the motto, "If you drive them to drink, drive them to Banjo's, where we aim to please, but once in a while miss." If you see Banjo, be sure to ask him how he got his name!

4 Buttes Supper Club is located 9 minutes west of Scobey at the Edge of the World. Bar is open 11:30-2 and restaurant serves 5-10. Owner Steve Frederick serves what many consider the best steak dinner anywhere and offers a great variety of other choices ranging from gizzards to lobster. Drinks available include a Buffalo Sweat and a White Shark and if you get to see Steve, ask about the outlaws that frequent the Buttes. Call 783-5318 for reservations.

EXHIBITS

Scobey Art Show on Main Street has good selection of oils, charcoal, pencil drawings, sculptures and much more from artists young and old of northeastern Montana. Call Barbara Hoffman at 487-5429 for details.

> **"Over 40 Buildings From The Turn Of The Century"**
>
> **Pioneer Town**

Pioneer Town at the west edge of town offers visitors a chance to see over 40 buildings and memorabilia from the turn of the century. Pioneer Museum features gun and antique car collections. Call 487-2224 or 487-5965 for details and hours. If you get a chance to meet Edgar, be sure to ask about the history of the area, he'll keep you entertained for hours.

HISTORIC PLACES

Whiskey Buttes and Outlaw Coulee west of Scobey are rich with colorful history of cowboys, Indian and outlaws during the whiskey running days of the early 1900's. Get directions and more information at the Museum or by calling 487-2224.

RECREATION

Scobey Golf Course on the SW edge of town is considered by many to be the best-kept secret in northeastern Montana. The nine-hole grass green course overlooks the Poplar River and offers enough water hazards and sand to make a challenging afternoon. Membership course is open to the public with reasonable greens fees and carts available. Club house has racketball facilities, hot tub, weight room and a lounge where you can celebrate your conquest of the course or lament your lost balls. Tee times available by calling Jim Heaton at 487-5322 or 487-2282.

SPECIAL EVENTS

Pioneer Days are held in Pioneer Town on the west end of Scobey during the 4th of July. Dirty Shame Variety Show features internationally known Dirty Shame Belles, Players and Dixieland Band. Variety show reserved seats go early so call for reservations at 487-5965 from 9-5. Special event highlights antique car and tractor parade, kids carnival and pancake breakfast in the "cook car." Contact Edgar Richardson at 487-2224 for exact dates and details.

Scobey Country Showdown Battle of the Bands and Street Dance is held on Main Street. Bands from a wide area compete for a chance to go to Nashville. You'll enjoy all kinds of music, dance your shoes away and laugh till your sides ache watching the great "Outhouse Race."

Daniels County Fair is held at the fairgrounds every August. Show features good livestock and agriculture exhibits, 4-H Style Show, rodeo and night shows. This fair is a good one and draws crowds four to five times the population of the whole county. The night show features nationally known performer.

EMERGENCY INFORMATION

Ron's Wheel Alignment does lots more as owner Ron Audet usually has a mechanic available from 7:30-5:30. Call Ron at 487-5946 for an appointment or just drop in for a cup of coffee and the latest news.

Daniels Memorial Hospital and Medical Clinic is located at Main and 5th Ave, phone 487-2296. Clinic hours are 10-5 Mon.-Thurs. and 10-12 Fri. 24-hour emergency service available at 487-2296. Call 487-2700 for an ambulance.

Daniels County Veterinarian Clinic is located a mile west of town and is open 8:30-5 Mon.-Fri. and 8:30-noon on Saturdays. Get friendly, expert help by calling 487-2862 for an appointment, or 783-5202 in case of emergency.

SEELEY LAKE

Highway 83 winds through a beautiful valley with a chain of lakes cradled between the Bob Marshall and Mission Mountain Wilderness areas. Situated along "the shortest and most scenic route between Yellowstone and Glacier," Seeley Lake offers a unique blend of year-round recreational activities in a community filled with exceptional accommodations and congenial residents. Restaurants, motels, RV parks, gift shops, dude ranches, resorts and seven large National Forest campgrounds help welcome all who come to relax in the area's pristine beauty or play in the great outdoors. Timber stands as the leading employer with tourism growing as a fast second. Old timers love to retell stories of yesteryear - Anaconda Company mining camps, rich resorts and tales of Copper King retreats, the beginning of Smokejumper history - even mountain lion and bear encounters. Still connected to its colorful heritage, Seeley Lake is an incredible four-season paradise, offering the best in nature and affordable, gracious lodging and dining. Tourist information is available through the local Chamber of Commerce at 677-2880.

WHERE TO EAT

The Season's Restaurant is managed by Ed Bezanson and is a great example of how the strength and beauty of the West can meet elegance and refinement to create a wonderful dining experience. Offering gourmet food and fine wines, locals love to meet at Ed's popular Sunday brunch and watch deer graze outside the historic log lodge. Be sure you ask about the unbelievably rich desserts...and if you can't make up your mind, try the caramel flan. Phone 677-2777 for reservations and a wonderful experience.

"Unbelievably Rich Desserts"

The Season's Restaurant

D F Chicken and Lounge is open noon-midnight Wed.-Sun. and is operated by Kelly Piche. Whether you eat in or take out, Kelly's famous chicken is always great. If you'd like a change of pace, try the delicious oyster dinner.

Filling Station Bar and Restaurant is open 7 a.m. to 2 a.m.. Owner/operator Don Larson offers great food with delicious, hearty servings for breakfast, lunch or dinner in his spacious dining room. Locals highly recommend the great Mexican dinners.

Kozy Korner Bar and Cafe is owned by Don and Ruth Sylvester, open 5 p.m. till 2 daily and is located in a secluded mountain meadow only 15 minutes from town. To get there, take the Woodworth Road above Salmon Lake, and be sure to watch out for the deer that will be checking you out right beside the road. The trip is worth it as Kozy Korner is much more than a great diner. Local favorites are the tantalizing Kozy Kut Steaks and super hamburgers.

Lindey's Prime Steak House is owned by Bud Lindemer and offers a great view of the bay as you enjoy one of Lindey's remarkable steak dinners. When you see B.L. or son, Mark, be sure to ask how they happened to have a seaplane base just across the lawn at the lake shore.

WHERE TO STAY

Wilderness Gateway Inn, is the only AAA rated motel in the valley, has 19 units and features a large hot tub and spacious rooms. A warm welcome is given to all from the new manager, Royale Taylor. When you meet Royale, don't hesitate to ask about where to go and what to see when you're in the area. Call 677-2095 for reservations.

Double Arrow Lodge is a widely known and highly respected resort on Seeley Lake with 14 units, indoor pool, hot tub, tennis courts and driving range offering cross country skiing, horseback rides and snowmobiling in season. Great accommodations with plush, comfortable rooms and cabins. If you see the manager, Ed Bezanson, ask about the status of the new golf course that's proposed within walking distance of the lodge. One of those places where you'll wish you could keep coming back every year. Call 677-2777 for information or reservations.

> **"You'll Wish You Could Come Back Every Year"**
>
> **Double Arrow Lodge**

Seeley Lake Resort and RV Park offers nice lakeside accommodations with 8 cabins with kitchenettes and 10 RV spaces. Outstanding for family reunions or retreats, the resort offers paddle boat rentals for touring the lake or wearing out the kids. Call 677-2434 to make a reservation with manager Don Beaver.

Leisure Lodge Resort has 8 units and is located on the lake with its own boat dock, lounge and sandy beach. A well-maintained classic motel operated by Bonnie Geleman, the lodge boasts towering tamarack and ponderosa pine that provide a beautiful and comfortable setting. Call 677-2376 for reservations.

SHOPPING

The State Station, open 9-5 Mon.-Sat., is owned by Frank and Jerry Netherton. Located in an authentic State Station, the store has a great selection of top quality antiques, pottery, custom jewelry, fine clothing and art from successful Montana artists. If you get to meet Jerry, ask her for an ice cream novelty from the antique soda fountain.

Cathy's Quilts and Cloth, open 10-5:30 Mon.-Sat., is a real find if you're looking for fine fabrics and gifts from a lady who offers old-fashioned, personalized service to all. If you're going to be in town for a while, check into when Cathy will be teaching her unique craft again.

Seeley Lake Pharmacy and Floral, operated by Robert and Mary Ann Stefczak, is open 9-5:30 Mon.-Fri. and 9-3 on Sat. Mary Ann or Robert can fill your prescription needs and give you friendly assistance with a gift selection. You'll enjoy investigating the fresh flowers and beautiful silk arrangements on display in the Floral Room.

WATERING HOLES

The Saloon on Hwy 83 is owned by Harry Northey Jr. and offers a friendly, rustic setting. Patrons range from loggers to lawyers and all enjoy this saloon when they want to kick up their heels in celebration of the good times.

The Filling Station downtown is a nice spot to stop for a cool one and enjoy the antique filling station memorabilia. Owner Don Larson can be counted on to start a good political discussion as he pours you a drink.

EXHIBITS

Wapiti Lodge and Resort, owned by Ramona Holt, is open Memorial Day through Labor Day and available for tours by reservation only. The "old town" is a complete turn-of-the-century complex featuring a saloon, blacksmith shop, livery stable, marshall's and territorial land office, school house and teacherage, freight depot and church. Be sure to visit Camp Nine, an historic logging camp.

"Old Town Is Great Turn Of The Century Exhibit"

Wapiti Lodge and Resort

RECREATION

Fishing is something special on a chain of lakes all will enjoy. From the fall rush of Dolly Varden to Cutthroat, Rainbow Trout, Brook Trout and Kokanee Salmon, the Seeley-Swan is a year round angler's paradise. Take in the beauty of surrounding mountains while you fish through the ice or walk along picturesque mountain streams in warmer seasons.

Hiking is wonderful on miles of trails too numerous to list and located on both sides of National Wilderness boundaries. The solitude broken only by the occasional rustling of wildlife creates a sense of peace that will be treasured for all memory. Be sure to allow an extra day or two, as you'll definitely be tempted to stay longer than planned.

Boating is exceptional as the many lakes lure enthusiasts of all types of water sports. Waterskiing is unbeatable on glassy surfaces sheltered from the wind.

Hunting is special in this valley as the first tinge of gold in the tamaracks brings memories of the one that got away. Whitetail, mule deer, elk, bear, goat and mountain lion all prowl the secluded haunts of the Seeley Lake area and offer promise to all who come. Professional outfitters are readily available to supply all the comforts of home to their clients as they seek the hunt of a lifetime.

Snowmobiling is spectacular with miles and miles of well-groomed trails that make Seeley-Swan one of the best-kept winter sports secrets. You'll find locals quickly volunteer if visitors need a guide or just some companionship.

Cross-country skiing is excellent on groomed trails, well-marked according to the ability of those that enjoy this winter wonderland on skis. Definitely a destination of pure joy and beauty for anyone who wishes to try this great sport in the land of Seeley-Swan.

"Wonderful Trail Ride-Float Trip Combination"

Double Arrow Outfitters

Horseback Riding is available at many resorts in the valley that offer recreational or trail rides. Jack Rich, head cowboy at the Double Arrow Outfitters can arrange for 1-2 hour rides, breakfast rides, wilderness rides, and even a trail ride/float trip. Doesn't that have a special appeal? Call 667-2317 to check out these options and more.

SPECIAL EVENTS

The 4th of July Celebration is special in Seeley Lake as the town explodes in a wide range of activities that include a parade, outdoor concerts and a dazzling display of fireworks over the lake. Campgrounds and lodging fill up well in advance, so call early for reservations.

Alpine Artisans is a local group committed to preserving and promoting Seeley-Swan area arts. It presents an art exhibit during the entire month of August downtown at the Stage Station. Contact Jeanne Moon at 677-2892 for more information.

Winter Carnival, held the first week of January, has a special outdoor winter parade you won't soon forget. Snow sculptures, dog sled rides and races, snowmobile races/games and cross country skiing combine to make this an energetic and festive way to begin the new year. Contact Marily Vinkemulder at 677-2724 for details on how you can participate.

The Seeley Lake 200, at the end of January opens the dog team race season in Seeley Lake with a four-day, out-and-back event that makes for great viewing. Competition is international and you'll enjoy the excitement close up as you watch the dogs harnessed up in a frenzy of barking and anticipation. For information on this special event, call Mary Anna Rich at 667-2460.

Race to the Sky is usually held two weeks after the Seeley Lake 200. It begins in Helena and uses Seeley Lake as one of its four stops. An unusual event, but very exiting to follow if you join the news crews as they watch the teams come in and listen to them relate stories of the miles just covered. Mary Anna Rich can give you times and places if you call 677-2460.

Snowmobilivous is held during the President's Day weekend in February each year and is a carnival of snowmobiling fun, games and prizes. Nighttime fun rides are always something to remember. The event is spon-

> **"Snow Sculptures And Dog Sled Rides"**
>
> Winter Carnival

sored by the local Snowmobile Club and more information is available by calling Derk Vinkemulder at 677-2724.

Hot Air Balloons come to Seeley Lake during the month of August. Get a new perspective of the chain of lakes in one of the most breathtaking rides you can imagine. Donations for rides and other proceeds are earmarked for selected service organizations. Call Dan Mizner at 677-2520 for details.

"Breathtaking Rides"

Hot Air Balloons Every August

EMERGENCY INFORMATION

Glen's Automotive on Hwy 83 offers reliable service for your vehicle at 677-2141 and owner Gen Morin is a great source of local information as well.

SOS Health Center is open from 10-5 Mon.-Fri. with a full-time doctor on staff. After hours call 677-2277 or dial 911 in case of emergency. Nearest complete emergency facilities are in Missoula, 50 miles by road or 15 minutes by Life Flight.

Seeley Lake Veterinary Service on Hwy 83 downtown is open 9-12 and 1-4 1st and 3rd Tuesdays Nov.-April and every Tuesday May-October. Dial 677-2550 for an appointment or 872-8339 in case of emergency.

TERRY

Cradled between the Yellowstone River and I-94, Terry offers all the amenities of small town Montana where a population of 600 friendly folks seem to always extend their hands to travelers in Big Sky Country. Farming and ranching provide economic vitality for a community born when railroads pushed through the plains. Terry is the home of the famous Lady Cameron photos, offers great agates to those who search and outstanding hunting on the prairies surrounding town. Tourist information is available from Larry Bonds at the Interstate Cenex.

WHERE TO EAT

Overland Restaurant on Hwy 10 E. is a family restaurant operated by Chris Ueland and offers great breakfasts and burgers served by friendly waitresses. If you see Glenda, ask her to fill you in on some fun things to do while you're in town.

Roy Rogers, located downtown on Hwy 10, is operated by Gary and Phyllis Twiford and is a favorite eating spot for lots of locals. Specialties include the small steak and pizza.

WHERE TO STAY

Diamond Motel on Hwy 10 East, downtown, is owned and operated by Bill and Fran Fleckenstein and offers travelers clean rooms and modest prices. Call 637-5407 for a reservation.

Kempton Hotel, downtown on Hwy 10, is operated by Henry Schwartz.

Roy's Trailer Court and Campground is

a great place to relax under a shade tree after a long days trek.

WHERE TO SHOP

Reyman Hardware, at 210 Logan, is operated by Travis Reyman. The exceptionally well stocked store offers a good line of sporting goods and is a great place to get advice on local hunting and fishing.

Rogerson's Gift and Hobby, downtown on Hwy 10, is owned and operated by Edna Rogerson. Edna offers a good selection of both agate and Black Hills jewelry, as well as abundant fishing supplies. When you see her, be sure to ask about the local campground or where the agate hunting is likely to be best.

"Good Selection Of Agate Jewelry"

Rogerson's Gift and Hobby

WATERING HOLES

Roy Rogers Bar is a great local meeting spot and is described in the restaurant section.

Bud and Bette's Place on Laundry Avenue has good food and a large collection of Charlie Russell prints and Jim Beam bottles. If you see owner Bud Golpen, you'll find he's a great source of information about hunting in the area.

HISTORIC PLACES

Lady Cameron Photos are on display in the Ed Gaub Accounting Office and are available for viewing from 9-5. These highly publicized prints vividly depict early eastern Montana life and were made from the original glass negatives used by Lady Cameron.

Prairie County Museum located at 101 Logan Avenue is open for viewing by contacting Ruth Franks or Ivy Brubaker. Artifacts on display are well-presented and depict early days on the plains of eastern Montana.

RECREATION

Agate hunting is of particular interest in the area, although hunting and fishing along the Yellowstone River are a source of great satisfaction.

SPECIAL EVENTS

Terryyippee is held on the last Saturday in July and includes 5 & 10 K runs, street dance, tennis matches and Bar-B-Que. Contact Larry Bond for details.

4th of July Rodeo at the fairgrounds is a great small-town rodeo. Local contact is Lon Reukauf.

EMERGENCY INFORMATION

Either Varner and Dockstader at 637-5558 or Terry Ford at 637-5746 can provide reliable car repair in downtown Terry. Call Marvin Varner or Roy Smith for an appointment. Mechanics on duty from 8-5 most days.

The Prairie County Hospital has a Physicians Assistant available to provide emergency care by calling 911. Nearest fully equipped emergency room is in Glendive or Miles City.

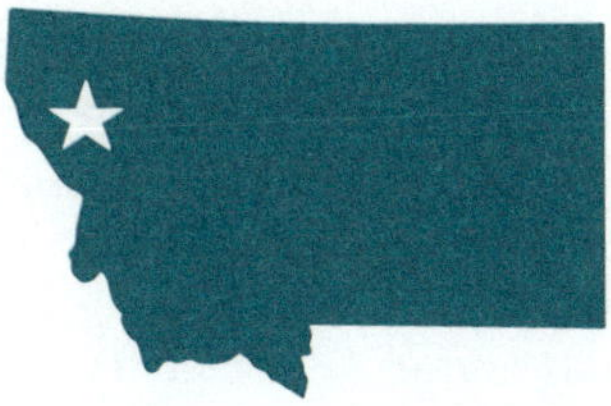

THOMPSON FALLS

In 1809, explorer and fur trader with the Hudson Bay Company, David Thompson, established the Salish House east of Thompson Falls, the first trading post in the area. In the mid 1800's, the discovery of gold brought prospectors to the valley, and in 1885, John Russell bought 40 acres and laid out the initial plan for the townsite of Thompson Falls, which had by then become a stop on the Northern Pacific Railway line. In 1905, Sanders County was created in the new state of Montana and named Thompson Falls as its county seat. In 1907, a courthouse and jail were constructed as the town bustled with activity and that old jail now houses the popular and interesting "Old Jail Museum." In 1913, the construction of the dam and power house began and both remain as popular attractions and examples of unique engineering projects of the period. Mining was a dominant activity in the early days, but timber and agriculture now sustain the community. The serene and majestic rivers, lakes, streams still combine with abundant wildlife and towering mountains to entice an ever-increasing number of visitors to the area. Tourist information is available from the Thompson Falls Chamber of Commerce at 4907 Hwy 200 in the Riverfront RV Park, or by calling Walt Haynes at 827-4930.

WHERE TO EAT

Granny's Homecooking at 915 Main is owned by Kathleen Pavilik and managed by Joanie Eichert. You'll find friendly service and homestyle cooking everyday at Granny's, where the locals like to gather to discuss what's going on in the area. Biscuits and gravy are a favorite for breakfast, and you're advised never to pass on the homemade

> **"Bisquits And Gravy Are A Favorite"**
>
> **Granny's Homecooking**

pies for dessert. If you See Joanie, be sure to ask how her horses are doing.

Rimrock Lodge at 4946 Hwy 200 is a mile west of town. Manager Ed McCune offers visitors an outstanding view of the Clark's Fork River as they enjoy fine food and old-fashioned western hospitality. If you see Nanny, the resident raccoon, she's not greeting you, she's holding out her hands for goodies!

Lonesome Dove Restaurant at 712 Main is open 11-2 Sundays and 12-8 Tue.-Saturday and is owned and operated by Dick and Billie Wells. The great atmosphere combines with outstanding wild game dinners to offer visitors a truly unique dining experience. Specialties include homemade soups, pasta, crepes and, of course, the savory taste of elk. If you see Dick, he'll be happy to share some great hunting adventures with you. Don't miss the antique shop in the back. Call 827-4337 for reservations.

"Wonderful Wild Game Dinners"

Lonesome Dove Restaurant

WHERE TO STAY

Falls Motel at 112 South Gallatin, has 22 units and a good location just two blocks from downtown and one block from the Clark's Fork River. This clean, comfortable operation is run by Marcia and Leonard Heiderscheidt and offers cable TV, HBO, exercise room and a soothing hot tub. Call 1-800-521-2184 or 827-3559 for reservations.

Rimrock Motel, located at 4946 Hwy 200 a mile west of town, has 25 units and is operated by Ed McCune. All rooms have great view of the river and satellite TV. Rimrock Restaurant is next door. Call 1-800-772-7312 or 827-3536 for reservations.

Birdland Bay RV Resort is located at 171 Blue Slide Road, three miles west of town off Hwy 200 at the head of the Noxon Reservoir on the Clark's Fork River. RV park with 17 large spaces and full hookups offers over a half mile of waterfront for fishing with boat dock and pedal boat rentals available. You'll love the beautiful 2 acre pond with in a quiet, secluded setting, great scenery and lots of wildlife. Owners are Joe and Jeanne Sol and hosts Dave and Karen Fitzwater take good care of your needs. If you get to meet Dave, ask him to relate the "charging moose" story.

Riverfront RV Park, at 4907 Hwy 200 has 10 spaces. Owners are Walt and Betty Haynes and facility offers dump station, showers, restrooms, convenience store with lodge and sleeping cabin available if you show up early. If you're not camping, it's worth a stop just to view the collectibles on display in the store. If you're going to be around for awhile, be sure to ask Walt or Betty when they're having their next auction. You won't want to miss it.

WHERE TO SHOP

Linda's Montana Gifts, at 1213 Main St., is open 9:30-5:30 Mon.-Saturday. Owner Linda Elliot has one of the largest Made-in-Montana selections in

the state that includes Indian beadwork, pottery, furniture and more. If you see Linda, ask her about the fun things to do in Thompson Falls; she always knows about the "good stuff."

The Outback at 919 Main is owned and operated by Jim and Bonnie Krogman, and is open to serve you 9-6, seven days a week. A great one-stop hunting, fishing and archery store. If you get to meet Jim, you'll find him a great source of information on where to find the big ones.

WATERING HOLES

Mother Lode Casino at 809 Main is operated by Dave and Bonnie Schroeder and offers great nighttime entertainment with pool tables, gaming machines and occasional live music on weekends. If you see Dave, ask him how successful he was on his last trip to Vegas.

Black Bear Bar at 919 Main is operated by Elsie Yates and offers what many locals consider to be the best paying machines in town.

EXHIBITS

Bighorn Sheep Viewing Station is located about 5 miles east of town on Hwy 200 and offers easy pull-out area for cars and RVs with information available at the stop. Great place to get photos of Bighorn sheep. Best season to view is winter through early summer, although they can be seen year round.

HISTORIC PLACES

Old Jail Museum in located on South Madison Street behind the Sheriff's office. Open Mother's Day till Labor Day, 12-4, seven days a week, the two-story brick building was built in 1906 and used as the Sanders County Jail until 1980. In the early days, the sheriff and his family lived in the first floor with the prisoner cells upstairs. The building is on the Montana State Historical Register and now houses the museum. Contact Sherry Hagerman-Benton or Joyce Bybee for more information.

Black Bear Hotel is located at 919 Main. Built in 1907 by Ed Donlan, it was originally called the Ward Hotel and is now owned by Elsie Yates.

RECREATION

The U.S. Forest Service at Thompson Falls and Trout Creek has free maps and brochures describing wilderness hiking and fishing opportunities in the area. Follow the highway signs to the Thompson Falls location or find the Trout Creek location just over the bridge on Hwy 200. You can actually arrange to spend a night or two in a remote fire lookout on top of a mountain; a wonderful experience and great place to watch the eagles soar and animals roam. Bring your camping gear and sleep inside one of the cabins.

> **"Spend A Night Or Two In A Remote Fire Lookout"**
>
> **U.S. Forest Service**

Flatiron Recreation Area is located two miles west of town on Hwy 200. The new boat launch is a great addition to picnic area and dock. This is a great place to catch that big bass, swim or just lay on the beach. Restrooms are available.

Prospect Creek Snowmobile Trails allow visitors to spend a day or a week exploring the high country in winter's splendor. Miles of groomed trails allow you to literally ride to Kellogg Idaho for lunch and back to Thompson Falls for dinner on some of the best trails in the West. Still one of Montana's best-kept secrets.

Thompson Falls Golf Course is located 2 miles west of town on Blue Slide Road. The great nine-hole, par three course is small, but challenging and offers beautiful play along the Clark's Fork River amid lush forests with fragrant scents and wildlife everywhere. Call 827-3438 for a tee time or more information.

Wild Goose Landing is situated 1/2 mile east of town on Hwy 200. Dock allows convenient access to lake and Clark's Fork River with restrooms and picnic area close by. Great spot for fishing, swimming or water-skiing.

SPECIAL EVENTS

The 4th of July Celebration is good time with parades, games, arts and crafts, fireworks and great food. Contact Walt Haynes at 827-3460 for details.

The Christmas Bazaar is held on the first Saturday in December at the Thompson Falls High School. Wonderful arts and crafts are offered for sale and great food abounds. Ginny Dyer can answer questions about this event at 827-4538.

> **"Wonderful Crafts And Great Food"**
>
> **The Christmas Bazaar**

The Huckleberry Festival is held in the town of Trout Creek during the second week of August. Trout Creek is just 15 minutes west of Thompson Falls on Hwy 20 and is known as the Huckleberry Capital of Montana. Three days of events enjoyed by all and include a fun run, games, arts and crafts. Jean Hannam can help with more information at 827-4835.

ENERGENCY INFORMATION

Doug's Towing and Auto Repair can provide full service auto repair and 24-hour towing. Doug Grimm is the owner and can be found at 4890 Hwy 200 or 827-4387.

Dr. Randy Lovel, D.O. is available at 907 Main to help with health problems. Regular office hours are 9-5 Mon.-Fri. and 9-12 on Sat. For appointments, call 827-4307. If care is needed after hours, this doctor actually makes house calls and can be reached at 827-4593. Nearest fully-equipped emergency room is 25 miles away in Plains.

Your pet will be safe in the hands of Dr. Gregg at the Thompson Falls Lynch Creek Vet Clinic located a mile east of town on Hwy 200. Regular office hours are 9-5 Tue. and 9-12 Wed. Call 827-4305 for an appointment or contact the Plains office after hours at 826-3235.

TOWNSEND

Townsend is known as "The First City on the Missouri" and located about half way between Yellowstone and Glacier Parks at the junction of US 287 and US 12. Tucked under the Elkhorn Mountain range in the Missouri Valley, many consider the area a sportsman's paradise. Townsend is only 5 minutes from great fishing and just 15 minutes from some of the finest bird and big game hunting in the country. Visitors will enjoy stops at any of four beautiful city parks, a museum or nine-hole golf course. The agriculture and timber based economy is supplemented by mining, small manufacturing, tourism and a good sized group of the town's 1600 residents who bring paychecks from work in Helena, 34 miles to the west. Tourist information is available at the Townsend City Hall, 127 S. Spruce, or by calling Dianna Mell at 266-3911. Other locations include Big Sky Electronics at 200 Broadway, Townsend Body Shop at 110 Broadway and the Mustang Motel at 412 N. Front.

WHERE TO EAT

Fireside Lounge is a mile east of town on Hwy 12 and offers a great salad bar and outstanding soup. Locals say they've never had a bad meal from owner Bob Chamberlain and daughter Leah. Steaks and the halibut special are highly recommended and Sunday Brunch is something you won't soon forget. For reservations or information call 266-3516.

Deep Creek Restaurant is 11 miles east of Townsend on Hwy 12 and offers gourmet dining in a log building. You'll be surprised and pleased at the menu and wine list offered by owner Jim Buckley. Don't miss the Sunday Brunch if you're in the area. Call 266-3718 for reservations.

Rosarios can be found at 310 N. Front and offers real Italian food you'll love in a unique remodeled service station. The food and decor created by owner Ron Burnetto will amaze you and you can't miss with the chicken parmesan, veal steak or stuffed shrimp. Phone is 266-3603.

Jasper's Pub and Pizza, at 216 N. Front, is owned and operated by Nathan and Gwen Bieber. Kids are welcome at this great family diner. The pizza is excellent and you'll never walk away hungry when you order a sandwich or broasted chicken. Specialties include chicken strips with JoJo's and Broadwater Pizza.

Horseshoe Family Dining is located at 500 Front Street and offers relaxed, homey atmosphere and reasonable prices. Operated by Steve and Colleen Ward, the locals highly recommend the great soups, prime rib sandwich and taco salad.

Yummies is the name and yummy is the game at 321 Broadway where Sarah and Ron Rogers' cafe and bakery feature great home cooking. You can't go wrong with the daily special and the baked goods are ....yummy! Open 6 A.M. until 2 P.M. except Sundays and for you breakfast buffet fans, Sarah's is on Saturday, and it's super.

WHERE TO STAY

Bedford Inn is a Bed and Breakfast located 3 miles north of town on US 287. Pete and Cheryl Rust have five units in a large home built in 1917 near the site of farmer Bedford Stage Station. You'll particularly enjoy the antiques and Pete's cooking; he's a chef, and he's good. Call 266-3629 for reservations.

"Pete's A Chef... And He's Good"

The Bedford Inn

Mustang Motel at 412 N. Front Street has 22 units and owners Iwy and Sharon Obrigewitch will give you the low-down on what's happening around the area.

Lake Townsend Motel at 413 N. Pine has 12 units and is operated by Stacia Wogamon. Housekeeping units are available also and be sure to check out the interesting local crafts in the office.

SHOPPING

Francisco Pharmacy and "The Gift

Shop" can be found at 223 Broadway. Owner operators John and Kathy McNulty offer super service and a great selection of gifts.

Big Sky Electronics and Floral at 200 Broadway is run by Neal and Barb Shaffer. In addition to appliance sales and service, the store offers a good selection of real and silk flowers, plants, and many local craft items.

Ace Hardware, at 204 Broadway, is operated by Paul Winslow. If you see him, get him to share some local gossip on anything involving sports.

WATERING HOLES

Mint Bar, Cafe and Hotel at 305 Broadway is operated by Mike and Jim Roe. It's a good place to meet the locals and enjoy good food. (Rotary meets here.)

Silo's Inn is located 7 miles NW of town on US 287. Owners Bill and Charleen Adams offer exceptional prime rib and generous servings. You'll enjoy friendly folk and a comfortable place to play a poker machine or two. Call 266-5622 for reservations.

> **"Exceptional Prime Rib"**
>
> **Silo's Inn**

EXHIBITS

Broadwater County Museum, at 133 N. Walnut, is open the middle of May through the middle of September, from 12:30-5. The museum is operated by the local Historical Society and you'll enjoy interesting displays ranging from pre-history of the area to Pat Duffy of Dallas, a native son.

Tori Jane's Antiques at 601 Broadway is owned and operated by Vern and Tori Jane Marion and offers visitors a look at an old refurbished school house that has been converted to an antique store. You'll find everything you can think of and some things you've never heard of in a nice setting. Call 266-4344 for hours or details.

RECREATION

Wildlife Viewing Area is located 1 1/2 miles north on N. Harrison at the corner of Canton Lane and Delger Road. You'll enjoy the whitetail deer, geese, and much more in this beautiful spot.

Old Baldy Golf Course is located a mile north of town on N. Harrison and offers nice nine-hole course with carts available and reasonable fees. No phone available.

SPECIAL EVENTS

July Festival features an antique car show, flea market and quilt show with food, music and fun. Held at the elementary school on N. Spruce during July, you'll really enjoy this special brand of small-town fun. Call Frank Ebert at 266-3453 for details.

> **"Antique Car Show, Flea Market And Quilt Exhibit"**
>
> **July Festival**

Broadwater Rodeo and Fair is held at the end of July, offering a local rodeo, a NRA event, Bar-B-Que, entertainment and livestock show. Fairgrounds are one mile east of town on US 12. Contact Elaine Graveley at 266-3443 for more information.

EMERGENCY INFORMATION

B & E Service at 302 N. Front can be counted on for reliable car or RV service. Owners Ed and Blondie Kaminski have a mechanic on duty 9-5 and can be reached at 266-3142. Wrecker service is available also.

Broadwater Community Health Center and Family Medical Clinic is located at 110 N. Oak and has office hours from 9-5. Call 266-3186 for an appointment or help after hours and 911 in case of emergency. Three doctors are on call at the hospital and local dentist, Matt West, is available at 415 Broadway or by calling 266-3402.

Your pet will get good care at the Elkhorn Veterinary Clinic located at the north end of town on Hwy 287. Office hours are 8:30-5:30, phone 266-5794. In case of emergency call 266-3510.

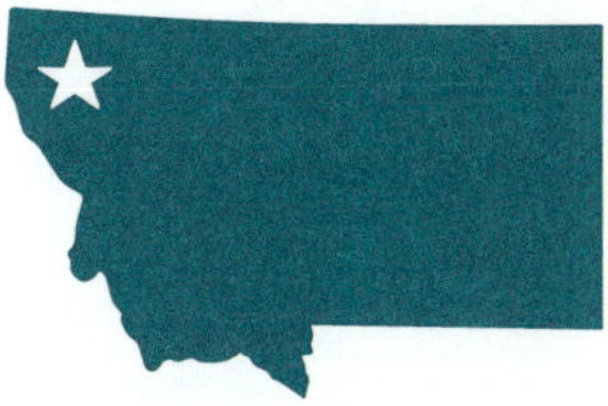

TROY

Nestled in the beautiful Rocky Mountains, you would never guess Troy has the lowest elevation in Montana. Summer and winter recreational opportunities abound including cross country skiing, snowmobiling, hunting, fishing, rafting, back-packing, swimming or wilderness trail hiking to picturesque camp sites. Primary employers in the area are the U.S. Forest Service, Asarco Mining, and the lumber industry. Troy boasts all the advantages of small-town living with good schools, and neighbors who take time to stop and chat, all in the middle of the timeless treasures of nature. Tourist information is available from 8-5 at the Troy Chamber of Commerce or by calling Larry Watt at 295-4216.

WHERE TO EAT

R-Place Restaurant and Drive Thru is located on Hwy 2 and is open from 10-10. This great family restaurant is operated by Greg and Bobbie Parent and offers good food in a nice atmosphere. Locals recommend the fish 'n chips with clam chowder, or the double bacon cheese burger with onion chips.

Silver Spur on Hwy 2 is open at 6 every morning. Owned and operated by Iris and Jim Sparksman, locals say it always offers a meal you can count on.

Gold Rush on Hwy 2 is managed by Joe Schmide and Glenn Cos, and is open 7 a.m. to 9 p.m. seven days a week. Great full-service restaurant.

Senior Citizens' Center is located at corner of 4th St. and Kalispell Avenue and

"Locals Recommend The Fish 'n Chips With Clam Chowder"

R-Place Restaurant

is managed by Paula Smith. Dinner is served on Tuesdays and Thursdays, but hours can vary so call 295-4140 for more information.

WHERE TO STAY

Holiday Motel has 6 units at 213 E. Missoula Avenue and is run by Roy Richardson at 295-4117.

Kurtz Lodging and Pool on old Highway 2 has two cabins along with a swimming pool, hot tub and weight lifting equipment. Call owners Rose and Lou Kurtz at 295-4630 for reservations or more information.

KOA Campground at 2898 Highway 2 has 50 camp sites, (15 full service, 15 elec/water) with 40 to 50 more for tents. Owners Danny and Marle Miller have showers and laundry facilities with many spaces located right on the river. Call 295-5959 for reservations or details.

"Many Spaces Right On The River"

KOA Campground

SHOPPING

Western Art Gallery at 1508 Hwy 2 West is operated by Rosalie Cox. Nice selection of western art, porcelain and scratchboard carving in a pleasant setting. Call Rosalie at 295-4748 for hours and specifics.

Kootenai Drug and Gift located on E. Highway 2 is open 9-6 Mon.-Sat. and 10-5 Sundays. The gift shop with full-service hardware and pharmacy is operated by Jim Seifert.

WATERING HOLES

Trojan Lanes on Hwy 2 is owned and operated by Ted Pacheco and offers good dining and a nice lounge casino next to the bowling alley.

Boondocks at 407 N. 2nd Avenue has a lounge and casino along with restaurant offering breakfast, lunch and dinner. Call Rod Johnson at 295-5780 for more information.

The Club Bar at 208 E. Yaak is operated by Tony Brown and has an open poker table.

EXHIBITS

Troy Museum and Visitors Center on Hwy 2 is open 11-5 seven days a week, from Memorial Day to Labor day. The museum has a nice display of historic exhibits from Troy and the surrounding area presented in a rustic building in hub of town. Call 295-4239 for more information.

Western Art Gallery at 1508 Hwy 2 West has a good selection of a wide variety of art in a pleasant setting. See more details in shopping section.

The Christmas Tree at the corner of 2nd and Kootenai is the largest living Christmas tree in the U.S. and has been lighted at the Christmas season since 1927. Contact local Chamber at 295-4216 for time and date of lighting ceremony.

"Largest Living Christmas Tree In The U.S."

Corner of 2nd and Kootenai

Swinging Bridge on Hwy 2 is situated over the Kootenai River and offers a beautiful view of Kootenai Falls. Nice picnic area with good fishing in picturesque location.

RECREATION

Kootenai River Outfitters, operated by Cliff Dare, offers very special excursions on the Kootenai River. Whether you want good fishing or spectacular subjects for photographs, you won't be disappointed with Cliff's expertise. Call 295-4487 for details and reservations.

SPECIAL EVENTS

The 4th of July Mining Festival and Celebration is good old-fashioned fun in the city park with a carnival, food booths, parade, exhibits, live music, fireworks, and literally something for everybody. Call Andrea Shaver at 295-4216 for details.

The Annual Big Sky Rendezvous is held in August at the Halfway House on Bull Lake Highway 56. A great country music festival with on-site camping available, children's activities and water sports facilities nearby. Good food and lots of smiling faces. Contact Billy Joe or Linda Davis at 295-4358 for more details.

Yaak River Raft Race is held on the Yaak River near Troy every year. A great escape and exiting event. Call

"Great Country Music Festival"

Big Sky Rendezvous

Mary Heim at 295-4561 for more information.

EMERGENCY INFORMATION

US Highway 2 Lube and Tire at 303 E. Missoula Avenue will take good care of you as Phil Fisher and Kelly Jillesed are available with mechanic on duty from 8-6 Mon-Fri and 11-3 on Saturday. Phone is 295-5948.

St. John Lutheran Hospital is located at 350 Louisiana Avenue in Libby, hours are 8-5. Call 295-7761 for an appointment or dial 911 in case of emergency.

Vet services are available in Libby also, and you can count on Paul Schaumberg for expert assistance at 2624 Hwy 2 South. Call 293-3717 to set up an appointment or arrange for service in Troy every other Wednesday.